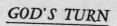GOD'S TURN

GOD'S TURN

by

HENRY SLOANE COFFIN

1934
Harper & Brothers Publishers
NEW YORK AND LONDON

God's Turn

CONTENTS

I

GOD'S TURN

"A God who worketh for him that waiteth for Him."—
Isaiah 64:4.

THE outstanding spiritual fact of our day is the shatter-
ing of men's self-confidence. The chief article in the creed
of the nineteenth century and the first part of the twen-
tieth was "I believe in man." Think of Emerson's essay
on "Self-reliance": "Trust thyself: every heart vibrates
to that iron string." Think of Walt Whitman's "Song of
Myself," beginning grandiloquently with the line

I celebrate myself, and sing myself,

and coming to its climax with:

And I say to mankind, Be not curious about God. . . .
I hear and behold God in every object, yet understand
    God not in the least.
Nor do I understand who there can be more wondrous
    than myself.

Think of the scientists and educators and idealists, who
believed that the Millennium was just around the corner,
and that we men were entirely competent to push the
world into it. And of all the optimistic people under the
shining sun we Americans were the most self-assured.
We in this best of all lands had the wisest institutions and
were the kindliest and most enlightened of all peoples.
Most of us believed in God whose providence had ordered
our lot so favorably; but our practical religion was "God

I

helps those who help themselves," and this last we were convinced we could do.

The War shook some of us to our foundations, but the great mass of our people recovered quickly, and in an orgy of optimism saw nothing but rosier and rosier tomorrows. These last years with the chaos in our economic life and in world affairs have blotted out those confident horizons. We are whistling to keep our courage up. Uncertain of ourselves, by no means assured that the cleverest minds can guarantee a happy future, aware that we understand next to nothing of this mysterious existence in which we take part for some brief years, there is a wistfulness for something above man—God or whatever other name may be employed.

A typical figure of the generation just passing is a writer of biographical sketches, Gamaliel Bradford, a part of whose daily journal has just been published. Bradford in earlier days had written very lightly of religion. He has a poem entitled "Exit God," in which he casually dismisses the Deity, although he concludes somewhat flippantly:

> I sometimes wish that God were back
>   In this dark world and wide;
> For though some virtues He might lack,
>   He had His pleasant side.

But after the War, in 1919, his diary contains this entry:

Who will tell me something of God? I know nothing about Him whatever. It is a mere name, a mere word to me, yet it clings. Why? Mere association brought down from my childhood and thousands of others'? Clouds and dreams and reveries, hopes and wonderings and fears? Or is there something deep and mysterious there that really takes hold of my soul? I cannot tell. But still the word clings to me, sometimes in the form of an oath, sometimes in that of an invocation or appeal, but still clings, and it seems to me that it grows.

GOD'S TURN

The prophecy from which our text is taken was addressed to a discouraged people. They had come back from their exile with the glowing hope of a new day, exactly as many of us during the War looked for an era of brotherhood at home and throughout the world. But their economic affairs were in a mess. The political situation was threatening, and another war might break upon them. Their religious institutions were languishing: "there is none that stirreth up himself to take hold of Thee." The tone of their public and private life was low: "We are all become as one that is unclean, and all our righteousnesses are as filthy rags." Their self-assurance was gone, and with a passionate longing they looked up:

> Oh that Thou wouldest rend the heavens,
> That Thou wouldest come down.

And the prophet declares his faith in a God whose distinctive characteristic is that He "worketh for him that waiteth for Him."

Would any of us have thus described God? To the majority of us He has been a God who waiteth for those who work for Him. Many of us have thought of the Bible as the record of man's progressive discoveries of the Unseen. God was conceived, like some vast continent lying afar, calmly awaiting the investigations of exploring men. Many of us have thought of Jesus as the most pioneering of men, whose faith took Him farthest and enabled Him to know clearliest the Invisible. We fancied God as waiting—waiting to be sought, waiting to be known, waiting to have men carry out His plans for their world. But in fact most people, even devout people, did not feel that God did very much. He had set this evolving cosmos agoing. He guaranteed its orderly continuance. But within the laws of its nature life went on: what men sowed they reaped. But there was no reaping apart from their sowing; nothing that came of itself. God's providence was seen in the response which answered man's effort. God did not initiate anything contemporaneously. Whatever got started was started by man. In the minds of not a few God seemed an elderly partner who had retired from active business and had left affairs in the hands of the sons of men. He had set a tradition to be lived up to, a code to be maintained. He was mildly interested in the outcome of this terrestrial venture and in its progress from day to day. But man was to go forward with the creation, and become creator of a new earth far superior to that which had been previously known. God would rejoice when His enterprising and conscientious children brought their Utopias to pass. Meanwhile He was waiting. That, I think, is not an exaggerated interpretation of American Protestant Christianity as it has been understood and lived by a fairly large number of earnest souls in our generation and its immediate predecessor. Our God was One who waits for those who work for Him.

As for ourselves, few of us are good at waiting. We wish to make events happen, and happen right away. Waiting upon Another does not appeal to us. We have stressed standing on one's own feet; we have prided ourselves on being self-starters (to employ the vernacular). And there is unquestionable value in independence and initiative. They are virtues, but virtues which if overemphasized lead to irreligion. To the self-reliant and self-starting man God becomes negligible, and a negligible God is obviously doomed to be discarded. Moreover, there are situations where these prized virtues are of no avail. Of what value is independence if one has been swept off one's feet by some tidal wave of circumstance, and finds no secure footing anywhere? Of what use to be an expert self-starter, if one is not sure whither to go? By and large our religion has been the shallow confidence in our-

selves of those who were floating comfortably on the flood tide of prosperity.

Happily our Christian heritage, coming from generations who sounded profounder depths, brings us the God of the Bible, who, unlike the well-nigh dispensable Deity of the attenuated faith of recent decades, is a God who worketh for those who wait for Him.

The initiative is always His. In every beginning God. Not only is He behind and in the cosmos—its originating Mind, its sustaining Life, its manifest Beauty—but if we know anything about Him, it is not because men boldly investigated and ferreted out this elusive Spirit. He has always been revealing Himself. Jeremiah graphically reports God as saying: "I spake unto you, rising up early and speaking." Men who were waiting listened and heard. Hence, the Bible and other divine words through the centuries. If we listen, a contemporary word comes to us from these utterances of long ago and in the events of today. The central fact in the Christian heritage is a Figure, a Man who lived by faith, who waited on His Father. But He did not think of Himself as originating anything. He spoke of Himself as One sent. His was a derived life, His work a mission from above. In all that He said and did, Another was present: "The Father abiding in Me doeth His works." And the Christian centuries have hailed Jesus of Nazareth as the supreme God-send, the Word made flesh.

The initiative in our fellowship with God always seems to us to be His. We love because He first loved us. "Thou wert long beforehand with my soul." None of us feel that we invited Him. He stood at the door and knocked. Through the circumstances of our childhood, through the best in our social heritage, through men and women who quickened us spiritually, through various events that have befallen us, God has pressed His friendship upon us. He is not the product of our wishful thinking. We may

at times call Him "our exceeding joy," but we should hardly use Bradford's irreverent phrase and say that He has "His pleasant side." So often He comes in the unwished-for—comes as Truth which we cannot help acknowledging, comes as inexorable obligation. He confronts us in life's inevitables—the grim things which must be accepted. He dogs us in responsibilities we would do almost anything to dodge. "Thou oughtest" sounds the inescapable voice of conscience. "Thou must" is its customary imperative. In Bradford's maturer phrase, God clings to us—clings in associations we cannot throw off, clings in memories not to be banished, clings through that haunting memory of a Life lived long since and dying on a cross and still living on—no mere memory but our most potent Contemporary. If we have personal fellowship with God, we feel that He began it and has almost entirely maintained it. "If we are faithless, He abideth faithful." He worketh even when we do not wait for Him.

If men have managed to achieve anything which gave them satisfaction, the best of them have not considered it their own doing. One might quote poets and novelists, inventors and explorers, who thought themselves voices and agents of Another. They agreed with Kipling's modest pioneer who opened a vast region for men to settle and grow rich in:

Anybody might have found it, but—His Whisper came to me!

Men who are consciously devout know that as they pursue their tasks, and are fatigued and depleted by the strain, they can find renewal—renewal in vision, in enthusiasm, in patience, in persistency. They look up, they wait on God, and He of whom they have sight, tirelessly and confidently going on, is their inspiration. "The ever-

lasting God, the Creator of the ends of the earth fainteth not." "My Father worketh even until now, and I work."

And as for social Utopias—a disarmed world, races purged of prejudice living together in mutual honor, an economic order where every man is secured the necessities for a full life—these are ideals born in men who waited on God. But in the plans and arrangements for their embodiment in human affairs—believing Christians do not identify their most wisely-contrived schemes with the kingdom of God. How boastfully many of us have talked of ourselves in recent decades as constructors of that kingdom, builders of the eternal city! We have projected our design, and then assumed that God was our Ally in its accomplishment. One hears utilitarian voices demanding that the forces of religion "line up" behind some measure of social reform or of international organization. We have been so sure that our idealisms, in the imperfect forms man's wisdom devised, merited cosmic backing. It has come perilously near to praying: Our will be done, and Thou shouldest align Thyself with us. We did not wait for God, we initiated and expected Him to work with us.

It is God's turn now. Most of our recent idealisms appear considerably damaged. That is no reason for abandoning ideals which have gripped us as from God. This is no time for cynicism or pessimism. These belong to pagans, not to believers in the God revealed in Christ. But we must recognize that we had assigned ourselves too lofty and too independent a rôle. We can tell ourselves as Robert Burns did the field mouse: "The best-laid schemes o' mice and men gang aft a-gley." The New Testament does not speak of men as co-creators with God of His kingdom, although we are fellow-workers with Him in it. That kingdom, according to Jesus, grows. It is an organism, like seed or leaven. Men can plant and cultivate, men can bring leaven into the mass of

dough; but God giveth seed and leaven, and their increase. Nor does the New Testament, like some recent hymns, call us builders of the eternal city. That city comes down from God out of heaven. He is both Architect and Builder. He worketh, and we wait upon His initiation and on His constant ordering of the process.

This does not relieve us of labor. Our prophet goes on: "Thou meetest him that worketh righteousness, those that remember Thee in Thy ways." They who wait on God are sped to errands of righteousness. And they remember God in His directed ways. There is a constant exposure of our ideals, and of our methods and designs, to His searching light. Only so do we keep working righteousness in a world whose circumstances change so swiftly that yesterday's righteousness may be today's iniquity. And while we work, God does not wait. "Thou meetest." He encounters us—often in judgment, condemning our righteous plans. That is how ancient good is seen uncouth. He meets us correctingly. We can all give instances of this in our own careers and in the idealistic movements of our day. He meets us mercifully, even through what seem to us disasters, clearing the way for better achievements no man foresaw. "God's gifts put man's best dreams to shame." And invariably God *meets* us. He has not withdrawn Himself from the highways and byways of earth where we move; He has not retired from this chaotic terrestrial enterprise.

Yes, it is God's turn. Man's self-confidence has been given a terrific jolt in these last years. This has been God meeting us, if we have eyes to see Him. We shall not be less eager to work righteousness. But we shall envisage our part in our Father's business more modestly. Walking humbly with God has not been characteristic of modern Christians. When so many of our hopes have crashed, and so many of our designs have worked badly or not worked at all; when we realize how impotent we

8

GOD'S TURN

are to control the civilization we prided ourselves on creating, and when that civilization itself is so unsatisfactory that there is no room left for pride; perhaps we shall talk less of ourselves as creators, and begin again to know ourselves creatures. "It is He that hath made us, and not we ourselves." "We are the clay, and Thou our Potter." Abraham Lincoln and devout folk of an earlier day habitually spoke of God as "My Maker." Instead of creators, we are at best tinkerers, sometimes helpful, sometimes blundering. Or, in New Testament language, we shall recall that we are children, not adults. One might diagnose the disease of humanity as premature adolescence. We suddenly got it into our heads that within this mortal life man could cease to be a child, and could get on by himself and control his own destiny. What rubbish has been written about being captains of our souls and masters of our fate and creators of an ideal commonwealth! Such talk bowed God out of His universe, and put man on the throne. We have not realized that in three score years and ten man does not pass much beyond the kindergarten stage, and that earth is populated by successive generations of children. Jesus assumed this even of the maturest pupils in His school, and said "I will not leave you orphans." Independence and initiative are virtues in children, and ought to be developed, but only up to a point, and they cannot be wisely developed except within the home, which rests on dependence and obedience.

It is not easy for us to wait upon Another, not easy for us to sing with Thomas Ken:

> Direct, control, suggest this day
> All I design, or do, or say.

Life's best things are never easily come by. Our times are supplying us with a stern discipline which is forcing us to wait. We must add to the compulsion of outward circumstance the self-discipline of holding ourselves at-

9

tentive and receptive to the living God. Our confident
crusades to create an ideal world have not resulted in
anything like that for which we hoped. It is high time
for us to return, or rather to advance, to basic New Testament Christianity, which insists that we become as little children and do not cease to continue as little children.
In this childlike relation of men with God, it becomes possible for Him to do exceeding abundantly above all that
we ask or think. To such, says Jesus, belongeth God's
realm. "Blessed are the poor in spirit, for theirs is the
kingdom of heaven."

SHIELDS OF BRASS

"And it came to pass in the fifth year of King Rehoboam, that Shishak king of Egypt came up against Jerusalem: and he took away the treasures of the house of the Lord, and the treasures of the king's house; he even took away all: and he took away all the shields of gold which Solomon had made. And King Rehoboam made in their stead shields of brass and committed them to the hands of the captains of the guard who kept the door of the king's house. And it was so, that, as oft as the king went into the house of the Lord, the guard bare them, and brought them back into the guardchamber."—I. Kings 14:25-27.

WHAT point is there in this incident of the brass shields with which King Rehoboam replaced the captured shields of gold? Why did the historian, drawing religious lessons from the nation's past, tell of these shields? Why is a detail like this part of the Holy Bible of the Christian Church? Has it anything to say to you and me?

Rehoboam was not a renowned monarch. Partly due to a situation which he inherited from Solomon and partly due to his own political blundering, he is rated as one of the failures under whom the national prestige was sadly lowered. He was brought up in the luxurious golden age of Solomon the magnificent. Under the surface of that prosperous reign there was growing social unrest which broke out at Solomon's death. The young Rehoboam was advised by older statesmen to make concessions, but the hot-heads of the younger generation were strong for

high-handed treatment of social radicals, and the new king stupidly followed their counsel. Most of his subjects rose in revolt and he lost more than half his kingdom. Judah and Benjamin were the only tribes which remained loyal to the house of David. So tiny a kingdom tempted attack from some great power. The Egyptian Pharaoh, Shishak, invaded it and Rehoboam could not resist his forces, and Shishak went off with the royal treasures. But Rehoboam had his father's golden shields copied in brass, and his guard carried them in the same state procession with which the people had been familiar in Solomon's day.

Is this historian laughing at Rehoboam when he recalled his guardsmen marching along with their shields of brass? Is he ironically contrasting his second-rate grandeur with the genuine wealth of his father? Quite likely. Even good people have an ill-natured way of smiling at those who are obliged to come down in the world and still hold their heads up proudly. But is not this the best thing that we know about Rehoboam that he did bravely keep up appearances? He had made a mess of his reign at the start, and committed an irreparable political mistake. He was powerless before Shishak, but he did not give up in despair. There were loyal subjects in Judah and Benjamin who stuck by him and wished him to remain their sovereign. Suppose he could not have a court with the same lavish display as his father's, he would give Judah as much splendor as he could. He would march with the same regal dignity, even if his guard carried shields of brass. And is not the middle-aged Rehoboam, accepting his limitations, continuing to govern his much diminished realm with the same attention to state functions which his father had shown, and holding himself just as majestically as he discharged his royal duties, a more admirable figure than the arrogant young sovereign of a wider domain? Is he to be laughed at? Are there not situations

in life for many of us when true nobility consists in keeping up and going on as though things were with us as they used to be when the bitter reality is that they are very different? Is not this a test which the years bring to not a few of us?

Here is a young couple who marry under the happiest auspices. Life for them fairly glitters with the gold of romance. The bride idealizes her young husband. In her eyes he towers a heroic figure with boundless powers, and she dreams of a distinguished career for him and for herself with him. And he looks at her through a golden haze, a queenly woman for whom nothing the world can offer is too splendid. Let us not be cynical about the shields of gold with which romance accompanies its beloved. These shining ideals with which lovers walk beside each other often have transforming power. A very ordinary fellow tries to be the royal husband his bride expects, and a very commonplace girl resolves not to disappoint her bridegroom's adoring dream. Marriage is meant to be a festival procession, in which man and wife walk through life with heads erect, proud of each other. Nor should life steal from them the gleaming shields of gold. Do we not all know elderly couples who go their way with impressive dignity because their love supplies unfailing mutual honor and admiration?

But when one or both feel that their life together is no such regal march, what then? Perhaps one has been foolish or worse, perhaps both have blundered and shown themselves unfeeling and inconsiderate, perhaps circumstances have drawn them apart and they seem to have nothing in common, and as they look at each other the shields of gold are no longer there. The wife realizes that she has married a mediocrity, or a weakling, or a scamp; the husband finds himself tied to a scold, or a bore, or a heartless worldling. The long years stretch out before them, and there seems no chance of change. In-

grained qualities of character are there, and there to stay. The glamour of their wedding-day will never be recaptured. Shall they go on and attempt to keep up the appearance of love, when their relations to each other seem a shabby make-believe of the golden radiance of their anticipation? Or shall they give up and add one more to the ever-mounting proportion of domestic casualties, which our social statisticians are recording as the ominous concomitant of present-day life? Is there not genuine nobility in following this ancient king, and reproducing the lost shields of gold with shields of baser metal as like them as may be? Suppose adoring love is impossible; suppose complete respect is out of the question; suppose even trust is difficult. Can shields be made of forbearing tolerance and a determination to hold a home together for children's sake and for society's sake? And can man and wife keep their heads high and maintain a dignified relation?

This is to walk with shields of brass, not gold; but with shields of brass one may fulfill social responsibilities. That is what Rehoboam did. Was it an easy thing for him to do? Was there not all manner of talk about him in Jerusalem, and much derisive laughter at the northern capital of Samaria? How tongues wag! A marital difficulty affords topics of as much gossip as the misdoings of any king. But as the years passed and Rehoboam went about his business, people became accustomed to the shields of brass. To be sure Rehoboam's reign was a come-down, but it was not a shipwreck. He kept the throne of the house of David when he might have abdicated. No one could call him a brilliant success, but Rehoboam discharged his royal duties with fidelity to the end, and transmitted a not dishonored crown to his son. Perhaps the shields of brass in time came to be not without a regal symbolism from their association with the steadfast dignity of a king who refused to be altogether beaten.

Here is a man who starts upon a career with sparkling

prospects. Possibly, like Rehoboam, he inherits position
and wealth; possibly, unlike him, he is born with large
abilities, and at school and college he is looked on as likely
to go very far. He has high ideals for his life-work, and
with a wide-open door before him his chosen calling shines
with golden promise. But somehow he commences badly.
Like our young monarch, he is ill-advised and he shows
poor judgment. Quite possibly, also like Rehoboam, he
may inherit from others a social situation which baffles
him. And a mistake in judgment for one prominent in
business or professional life is a costly matter. Young
ministers, young physicians, young lawyers, in responsible
posts, young men in places of trust in the commercial
world, cannot blunder, and escape dire consequences.
Their career can never be the same again. Their kingdom
in large part is taken from them irrevocably. There is
something cruel about the consequences of mistakes for
those in conspicuous positions. If they were subordinates,
they might be guilty of bad judgment and make a good
many blunders, and learn by their failures, and then arrive
in maturity in the confidence of men. But no such chances
of experiment are allowed a Rehoboam. If he fails, he
is severely judged, and his whole future career is
shadowed. The shields of gold are gone.

What then? Is not that the test which comes to many?
They have a tradition and genuine powers, and they have
partially failed. Shall they throw up their careers? Shall
they confess themselves defeated? Because Jeroboam and
ten-twelfths of Israel have no use for them, shall they
abdicate? That way lies suicide—the course of King Saul,
who, when the battle went against him, took his own sword
and fell upon it. Or shall they substitute shields of brass
for shields of gold, let people say what they will, and
accept a diminished opportunity, and go on fulfilling their
obligations to the community and doing its work? It is
hard for a man who has been governing twelve tribes

to come down to two. It is hard for a man who has been born to shields of gold, and who has seen them carried about him, to come down to shields of brass. Rehoboam has bitter hours when he has to fight to keep his own self-respect. But he has years ahead of him, and he has no right to deprive the remnant of his people of any service he can render.

All honor to those who have blundered and failed, and have won the ill opinion of men, and lost their high standing, but have picked up the pieces of their careers, and gone faithfully on to the end! History blows no trumpets for them. Solomon's is the golden day, theirs a day of much less prized metal. But it takes courage of no common sort to be much poorer both in possessions and in the esteem of men and still be kingly. Much of the luster is gone from the career, but the middle-aged and elderly man faithfully keeping up and keeping on is not contemptible.

Here is a man with a social conscience. He has his visions of more comradely industry and business, higher-principled politics, more fraternal international relations, more mutual honor and confidence between race and race. People smile condescendingly at the glowing idealism of youthful enthusiasts for a new world. God help us when our young men and women cease being critical of things as they are and serenely confident that they can hasten the Millennium. Of such hopeful souls is the kingdom of heaven. Well for our tough world that each new generation arrives on the scene carrying shields of shining gold. It is not a good thing when shrewd old Solomon manages affairs for the benefit of his own group, while thousands are forced to hard labor, bitterly resentful of his luxury. It is a worse thing when the Solomons breed a generation of insolent youths, who consider themselves born to privilege and have no sympathy with the aspirations of the unprivileged many. They are a more serious menace

to society than the reddest agitator. But when our idealist finds himself in a position of responsibility, where he must make practical decisions, how hard it is to keep his shields of gold! Here is Jeroboam stealing five-sixths of the people to worship false gods of material prosperity, and here is Shishak with his terrifying military power. Few men assume public office, like Rehoboam, and mix in politics and emerge still attended by golden shields. Few of us in administrative positions in business or education or even in the Church fail to discover that our ideals are seldom capable of being immediately realized. Think of the musicians and artists and men of letters whose careers have to be a series of compromises with the artistically illiterate!

Some idealists, if they cannot have their shields of gold, refuse to continue to serve. And there are situations in which they may be wise. But for most of us the problem is Rehoboam's. Ten tribes have gone off after Jeroboam—very well, we cannot mend that now. Here are Judah and Benjamin prepared to follow us: dare we desert them? Shishak is a force to be reckoned with, and we cannot have ideal conditions even in Judah while he dominates. Must not a man who would be both an idealist and a servant of this imperfect age make shields as like the shields of gold as he can make them, and carry on in the position where Providence has set him? He knows and everyone else knows that the shields are not gold. He wishes they were; but with Shishak and Jeroboam in power golden shields are not within his reach. Some successor, please God, will recapture them. Meanwhile, what can he do? Let him be faithful in his small realm with shields of the best metal he can command.

Or here is a devout soul who has been reared in a golden religious tradition of rich belief. God has seemed very real and very satisfying, and there have been no disturbing doubts. Life's every walk has been attended by

gleaming shields of religious conviction. But Jeroboam and Shishak have come on the scene, some movement of thought or some staggering personal tragedy has taken away the shields of gold. And Rehoboam is tempted to resign. Without these golden beliefs in a good God, in the spiritual nature of man, in the redeeming power of love, in immortal life, what is there to live for and work for? We ought to seek the richest faith—the pure gold of complete assurance. But the plain fact is that a great many people have to live with something else. It is such a very small domain of truth that any man possesses— too small to produce golden interpretations of a whole universe.

And even the greatest saints confess that they have hours when their shields of gold are gone. Many of the staunchest of them have to walk by the memory of yesterday's faith in the hope that it will come back to them tomorrow. Paul wrote—and I think he meant it of spiritual as well as of material riches: "I know how to be abased, and I know also how to abound: in everything and in all things have I learned the secret both to be filled and to be hungry, both to abound and to be in want." There are times when we have to admit that we have no shields of gold, our beliefs are improvised shields, the best we can contrive with our existing experience and knowledge. Paul learned how to be hungry and at the same time discharge his responsibilities, to be in want and still to serve the needs of others, to say, "I know in part and I prophesy in part," and still to prophesy. In this spiritual realm we are sure that ultimately both Jeroboam and Shishak are going to be beaten, and we are to have our golden shields. But this may not happen tomorrow or the day after tomorrow. Many earnest souls do not reach complete and abiding assurance; indeed, few do. Meanwhile under God there are kingly duties to be fulfilled. And there is something noble in the man who

goes his way accompanied by shields of brass, by not altogether satisfactory beliefs, but the best interpretations of God and man and the mysteries of life and death he can seem to reach under the circumstances.

Or, once more, here is a man or woman for whom life has supplied a golden companionship. In some friend who means everything to him, in son or daughter who really makes life for him, in the wife at his side who fills his days with love, he goes his way accompanied by shields of gold. But the ever-threatening invader comes and death takes away the beloved companion and his golden shields are gone. What heart-aching readjustments men and women have to make! How utterly bleak life seems to them! There is no use blinking the grim fact that their days henceforth are impoverished. There is no help in any comfort which does not face open-eyed the reality of their loss. Life for them as for Rehoboam, after Jeroboam's revolt and Shishak's invasion, is woefully different. And for them there come hours when they sincerely wish that they might give up. Without the golden companionship they knew, all things seem stale and unprofitable. But here are Judah and Benjamin, their responsibilities. Can they fail them? Do they wish to shadow their lives by giving over all the gay appearances with which they have been familiar? They have no resources of gold; but there is a fine courage in making shields of brass and insisting that life's routine shall go on with the old festivity. All honor to the lonely-hearted men and women who do not parade their sorrows, but rather give Judah and Benjamin the most regal service they can.

We have been thinking of a very unadmirable Old Testament figure of David's lineage; and before we close let our minds travel down the centuries to Rehoboam's greatest descendant. Readers of the Gospels find a period when Jesus goes His way accompanied by the golden shields of the enthusiastic loyalty of hundreds. His mes-

sage of the Kingdom of God seems to be capturing the popular heart in Galilee, and who can tell how this movement may spread? But the shields of gold are not with Him for long. The crowds have turned from Him, and eyeing the loyal few who remain, He asks: "Will ye also go away?" The only means in His power to establish His kingdom is to go up and offer Himself a sacrifice at Jerusalem. And He is not always sure that this costly effort will succeed. He passes through struggles of soul. People regard Him as a failure. His nearest friends shake their heads over Him. This desperate venture of love in vicarious sacrifice is not His own preferred plan. He pleads in agony for a golden alternative: "O My Father, if it be possible, let this cup pass away from Me: nevertheless, not as I will, but as Thou wilt." It is the courage of accepting what seems to Him a second best, of doing the only thing possible under circumstances when what He started out at first to do has failed.

And ever since all the blundering Rehoboams, who have lost large parts of their kingdoms and had their golden shields taken from them, come and put their unhappy situations beside that cross, and find in Him the Captain of the losing legion, the Comrade of those without reputation, the Leader of men reduced to life's second bests, the Saviour of sinners, and out of them He makes a hallowed company of kings and priests unto God.

III

THE CHRISTIAN CREED AND LIFE

"To us there is one God, the Father, of whom are all things, and we unto Him; and one Lord, Jesus Christ, through whom are all things, and we through Him.—
I. Cor. 8:6.

HAD the apostle been writing today, he might have said: "To us Christians there is at least one God." Early Christianity faced a world that worshiped many deities; we face a world disposed to worship none at all. Many share the feeling of Thomas Hardy that ours is "a nonchalant universe." "We enter Church," he confesses, "and we have to sing 'My soul doth magnify the Lord,' when what we want to sing is, 'O that my soul could find some Lord that it could magnify.'"

But, although there are few professing polytheists among us, there are the same confused and conflicting loyalties as prevailed among worshipers of gods many and lords many. An ancient Greek found it distracting to keep in the favor of Artemis and Hera and Pallas Athene. And today most people revere one idea in the home and another in business, seek truth in science and follow expediency in politics, admire beauty in nature and cultivate ugly utility in their cities, extol unselfishness in the dealings of man with man and insist on self-interest in international relations. Consequently their characters are things of shreds and patches—crazy-quilts of noble and sordid traits. To bring unity out of this moral chaos let

us at least look at this fundamental Christian conviction—
one God, and *one* Lord.

It is worth noticing that a Hebrew of Hebrews, like
this student of Gamaliel's, staunch in the monotheism of
his fathers, sets side by side in his worship one God,
the Father, and one Lord—a Man who had been executed
in Jerusalem thirty-odd years before, about the time he
was at college there. The divinity of Jesus was not a
dogma reached by speculative reasoning. These first generation Christians—some of whom had been companions
of Jesus in Galilee, and all of whom, like St. Paul, had
felt the transforming power of His cross and victorious
life—instinctively called Him Lord, and associated Him
in their trust and adoration with God. This was their
spontaneous response to Him. They were not lapsing into
polytheism with its distracting allegiances. Olympus had
its jealousies and quarrels, for that was the level of its
life; but in the Deity of Christian worship there was one
purpose, one motive, one nature—redeeming love. They
could be at the same time steadfast monotheists with one
God and worship Jesus their one Lord. Jesus and God
belonged together in their devotion, and gave them not
a divided but a unified life of love.

Today when we face Jesus of Nazareth—His life, His
death, His continuing power, when we recall what He
has meant century after century, when we remember what
He has been to ourselves, is there any place in our regard
too exalted for Him, any word in our vocabulary too high
for Him? However lofty our conception of God, is He
better than Jesus? Are we not constrained to offer Him
our utmost reverence and fealty so that we have naught
more to offer God? We are either idolaters, man-
worshipers, or Jesus belongs with God; and to be completely religious is to share this historic Christian faith
in one God and one Lord.

Our relationship to this God and Lord is expressed

in the prepositions which the apostle uses. These little words, which probably suggested themselves to him without his picking and choosing them, are like the bed of a brook—the inevitable course in which his spirit's life flows—of, through, unto.

"One God, the Father, *of* whom are all things." Writers on education today keep insisting that its main goal is to make students creative. St. Paul would not quarrel with that: he believed that he and his fellow-Christians were to be workers together with the creative God. But he was convinced that before anybody can create he must know how to derive. "One God, *of* whom are all things."

People talk about making a garden, but how steadily a garden keeps reminding us: "What hast thou that thou didst not receive?" The sandy subsoil that supplies drainage may be the moraine of a glacier of the ice age. The fertile elements in the dirt which our trowel turns are mold from long-decayed forests or the rotted leaves of former summers. The seeds and bulbs represent a long evolution of plant-life and their ancestry carries back to China, to the Alps, to the Caucasus, to Australia. The tools in our hands are products of the ingenuity and experience of numberless gardeners through the centuries. Our fertilizer may be the ground-up bones of animals. And the garden depends principally upon sunlight and moisture, neither of which we can create. To make a garden is to know how to be heir of a far-stretching past and to derive from the energies of the cosmos.

College students have the laudable ambition to contribute to man's knowledge and enrich his life. But take the man whom the age acclaims for his additions to human well-being, and on what can one set one's finger and say: "That was his creation"? Originality is our word for a good digestion. The man took, assimilated and made available what was at hand. When he surveys his own mind and itemizes what came to him from parents,

teachers, books, experiences, he hears the voice: "What hast thou that thou didst not receive?" Your really creative thinker humbly feels that he did not so much invent as derive.

The religious man, whether in his garden or his study, goes behind the happenings of the cosmos which bring him his materials and behind the thoughts of man which supply him with his knowledge to the Source, of whom are all things. Nor does he limit his deriving to the developments of the æons. If God be Father, he can have immediate fellowship with Him, and obtain wisdom, strength, life directly from the touch of Spirit with spirit. He makes his heredity contemporary. God's paternity for him is not merely a past event, but a present process. He lets God father his plans, his sympathies, his endeavors. He takes his interests and his motives from Him, he lives from God.

This is not to look at life in the first instance creatively but derivatively. It is not to say: "What shall I do with my college course; what shall I make of its friendships; how shall I manage the situations in which I find myself?" But to say: "This year's studies, friendships, tasks come to me of God; this I who enter the year am of God—the child of His thought and love; the resources which can supplement and alter me, enabling me to find truth through studies, friendship through contact with men, a divine purpose through the welter of experiences that befall me, are of Him. I will take tasks, self, resources from Him." This is the religious life—a constantly deriving life. Never fear but that it will also be creative. That was a suggestive tribute paid to Gladstone, the practicing believer, with his earnestness, enthusiasm, energy, abounding at four score years and beyond, by his biographer, the agnostic John Morley: "He lived from a great depth of being."

"One Lord, Jesus Christ, *through* whom are all things

and we *through* Him." It was through Christ that Paul
had found this enriching Father. His characteristic name
for Deity is "the God and Father of our Lord Jesus
Christ." To him God was the response from the Unseen
which answered the faith of Jesus; or the gracious Approach from the Unseen expressed in Jesus. Jesus was
the Transmitter of the life which he derived from God.
The autobiography of his struggles concludes: "I thank
God *through* Jesus Christ our Lord."

None of us would disparage what comes to him along
any avenue. God has numberless paths by which He en-
ters His world and comes to us. Paul never belittled his
pre-Christian heritage nor the spiritual possessions of
Greeks and barbarians who had never known his ancestral
faith. But the door through which that which matters most
to us came and still comes is the Figure of Galilee and
Calvary. There is a distinctive quality in those who say:
"We through Him." One cannot sum that quality up in
adjectives—loving, believing, daring and so on. All per-
sonalities defy description and this quality is the infec-
tion of a personality. Followers of Christ in every age,
from that First Century group whom Walter Pater de-
scribes at worship in Cecilia's house in Rome with something "from beyond the flaming ramparts of the world
already moulding anew their very bodies and looks and
voices," down to that English nurse of a few years ago,
feeding her soul on Thomas à Kempis' *Imitation of Christ*,
saying as she goes to be shot: "I see now that patriotism
is not enough; I must die without hatred or bitterness towards anyone"—followers of Christ in every age betray
qualities which suggest Him. These qualities are shown,
of course, under the conditions and in the forms of their
time. But they have a distinctive flavor which one associates with Christ. And it is not only the quality of their
life, but the power with which they live. Time after time
in history one sees mankind becoming morally decadent,

25

then recovering touch with this strange Figure, and acquiring a nerve and vigor to attempt the Christlike.

Just over the threshold of this academic year, if we commit ourselves to Jesus that He may control our purposes, there will be a quality in our work and our friendship, in the inner texture and outward impress of our characters, which will make us godsends. We shall be of God, the Father, through the Lord Jesus Christ.

"And we *unto* God." Many ethical thinkers would put before us as the goal of life the ideal human society. They would have us live with a just commonwealth before us, asking: "How will my acts look in the eyes of that friendly community?" It is a searching bar before which to give our account. No Christian can forget that he belongs to the vast brotherhood of God's children of every race and condition, and that he must be prepared to report to them his use of his portion of the family heritage—the spiritual and material goods at his disposal (and how much they total for each of us at a college like this!). Further, a Christian looks ahead to life in a land of light with citizens out of every kindred and nation, where what each *is*—and that will be the summary of all that he has felt, thought, dreamed—shall be manifest. This is the publicity of that world "where loyal hearts and true stand ever in the light." But our immediate accountability is neither to the collective humanity alive today, few of whom know us and none of whom can scan our motives, nor to the enlightened society of a remote tomorrow, but to God the Father of all. We stand today at the bar of His justice. We face always His love in that cross where a Life was laid down for all. We take life from Him; we account for it to Him. What men think of us today or on some more clear-sighted tomorrow is of little consequence. What God thinks of us is everything.

One evangelist introduces the scene in the Upper Room by picturing what passed in Jesus' mind: "Jesus, know-

ing that He came forth from God and goeth unto God,"
took a basin and towel, and washed His ambitious disciples' feet, and changed the anti-social atmosphere of
that circle into one of comradeship. That picture in the
mind of Christ—from God to God—is the picture to set
in our thoughts. To come to one's work, to one's fun, to
one's companions, to one's ordeals, from God, and to go
from them straight to His presence, will be to *socialize*
them (to use a word much prized today), will be to lift
them up to the heaven of God's love as that Upper Room
is the heavenliest spot we recall on our earth. This is the
direction in which we must keep turning ourselves: "we
unto God."

But someone here of the mood of Thomas Hardy will
complain that, after mentioning the difficulties modern
minds have with Christian faith, we coolly brushed them
aside and have spent our time exploring the convictions
of a long-dead apostle without seriously testing their
validity. Well, St. Paul was not arguing when he penned
this text, but asserting, and asserting on the basis of
spiritual discoveries which he and his fellow-believers had
made. *"To us,"* he begins, "there *is* one God and one
Lord." That is the way in which living, as opposed to
moribund, religion always speaks. It does not bolster
itself up with testimonials from scientists and philosophers
that it is intellectually respectable. It does not plead with
social reformers that it makes some small contribution to
human welfare, and ought, therefore, to be tolerated and
licensed in the ethical commonwealth. In the name of
the august Most High God with whom it has to do it
declares: "We speak that we do know; yes we speak as
though God did entreat you by us." And why should it not
so speak? Its assertions are reports, as honest as erring
human minds and tongues can make them, of *findings*.

A few weeks ago I happened to be with a group of
men who were seeking a water supply for a cabin in

27

the mountains. At the foot of the hill where the cabin was to be built, there was what had long been thought a small spring, from which ran a fairly steady trickle even on that mid-August day. But the men in the group were of various minds about it. One allowed that he had always heard that there was a spring there, but now that he looked at it closely he thought it might be just the drainage of the hillside seeping down towards the brook, whose almost parched bed lay below. Another, in corroboration of this doubt, called attention to the fact that there was not one trickle but several, and that they were some yards apart. A third thought that there was a spring there, and that it gave good water, but he questioned whether there was enough of it for the dependable supply of a household. But as no other source of water was available, and as this spot had the reputation of containing a spring, for a piece of pipe had been placed there by somebody years ago for the convenience of trampers who wanted a drink, it was resolved to begin digging and explore. The diggers were astonished, after some shovelsful of topsoil had been removed and they got down to sand, to discover how abundant the flow, and how the various trickles, when followed up, converged into a single pool. And when the spring had been walled up with stone and concrete into a well-hole with a capacity of forty-eight gallons, it filled completely in three-quarters of an hour on a day in the last week of a dry August.

Men have always needed and continue to need a fountain of life—a supply of refreshment and invigoration and cleansing. For untold generations there has been a report, surprisingly widespread throughout the race, that there is a Spring of living water in the Invisible. Wayfarers have told of their finding it and drinking of it. But today mankind stands before this alleged Spring expressing divers opinions concerning it. Some look contemptuously at the trickles, and declare them negligible

THE CHRISTIAN CREED AND LIFE

for humanity's present needs. Some assert that such
waters are injurious to social well-being—waters of Lethe
lulling to sleep amid economic injustices. Others do not
question that many in the past have slaked their thirst
here, but consider this no adequate proof that it is a living spring: it is the seepage of the spiritual idealism of
the times which credulous souls have mistaken for a peren-
nial flow. Others again point to the several trickles and
doubt whether they come from a single source. But there
continue to be a not inconsiderable company who regularly depend upon this Spring. While the rest are dis-
cussing it, they go on drawing from it. Surely their findings are the only evidence that matters.

And they (may I not put it into the first person for
this company and say, and *we*?) repeat the conviction
of this frequenter of the Spring centuries ago: "to us
there is one God, the Father, of whom are all things,
and we unto Him." And further, we share his conviction
that the various trickles converge to one pool where the
fullness of the religious inspirations of the race becomes
accessible to us, and then in some measure accessible
through us. We hear a Voice: "If any man thirst, let
him come unto Me and drink. He that believeth on Me,
from within him shall flow rivers of living water." This
is our "one Lord, Jesus Christ, through whom are all
things, and we through Him."

IV

FAITH AND FAITHFULNESS

"And Salmon begat Boaz of Rahab; and Boaz begat Obed of Ruth."—Matt. 1:5.

TRAVELERS in foreign lands who follow the beaten track are certain not to miss the principal sights; but there is a peculiar pleasure in leaving the tourist-crowded routes and visiting some seldom-explored district. The Bible has its frequented highways, where in well-known passages millions generation after generation find themselves face to face with God. But its little-read chapters also lead to Him.

No verses are more usually skipped than the genealogies. Some of us have wondered why they were put in to begin with, or why modern revisers had not the courage to delete them, or why publishers waste paper and printers' ink on pages which exist only to be passed over. A New England woman of the last century is said to have memorized the genealogies on the theory that she would meet these people in heaven and it was well to know their names beforehand; but we have no basis for her assurance about the destiny of some of them, nor do we know enough about them to be able to say that we should find them interesting to meet. And it seems peculiarly unfortunate that our New Testament should start off with a list of unpronounceable names, for persons unacquainted with this greatest of all books naturally begin at the beginning and become at once discouraged.

Our first Gospel was written for readers who had an

interest in ancestries. The evangelist wished to present Jesus as the lineal descendant of Abraham and David—the Heir of the best in Israel's past. And incidentally he introduces the names of four women, three of whom are Gentiles, which was perhaps this author's way of broadening his appeal, and suggesting that other blood than that of the chosen race flowed in this Life who was destined to be the Saviour of mankind. Two of these outsiders, Rahab of Jericho and Ruth from Moab, are in themselves interesting characters; and when found, as in this genealogy, side by side, they suggest some striking contrasts among those who compose the communion of saints, and in the methods by which God brings His children into line with His purposes.

Rahab was a degraded woman, plying an unspeakable trade in the city of Jericho. She is as depraved a creature as one can find in the entire Bible. She was a traitress to her city, lodging its enemies' spies. She lied brazenly. She contemplated without emotion the horrible slaughter of all her fellow townsfolk, men, women and little children. She displayed no feeling for a single neighbor or acquaintance. The only vestige of affection appears in her care for her family; and there is a pathos in the way in which this prostitute, self-debarred from a family of her own, names her kindred: "Swear unto me that ye will save alive my father, and my mother, and my brethren, and my sisters, and all that they have, and will deliver our lives from death."

One is surprised to find this woman commended not only by an Old Testament historian, whose patriotism may have run away with his conscience, but also by two New Testament writers, who include her among their saints. James speaks of her as a striking example of faith showing itself in works, and the writer of *Hebrews* places her in his list of notable believers immediately after the patriarchs and Moses. Think in what her claim to saint-

liness consists! She had heard of the conquering advance of an invading horde of desert clansmen, inspired with enthusiasm for their tribal god, Jehovah. Impressed with this Deity's superior power, and moved by fear, she espoused the cause of His devotees:

"We have heard how Jehovah dried up the water of the Red Sea before you, when ye came out of Egypt; and what ye did unto the two kings of the Amorites, that were beyond the Jordan, unto Sihon and to Og, whom ye utterly destroyed. And as soon as we had heard it, our hearts did melt, neither did there remain any more spirit in any man, because of you: for Jehovah your God, He is God in heaven above, and on earth beneath."

Unquestionably she had religious insight, but all that it did for her was to lead her to adopt a course of treachery and lying, and to drive a selfish bargain for her own and her family's safety. The woman's morals were abominable; but her faith was strong. And that faith saved her life, made her an ally of God and an agent in His purpose, gave her a place among His people, where afterwards she found a husband and a home, and a lasting name as an ancestress of kings and of Jesus the Christ.

Ruth was a Moabitish girl of attractive disposition and charming manners, who had married Mahlon, the son of a famine refugee from Judah, and had been left a young widow childlcss and with a lonely mother-in-law to care for. She is loyally affectionate and resolute in fulfilling her obligations. Her answer to Naomi, when she begs her not to go with her to a land of strangers, but to return to her own people, is the classic utterance of staunch fidelity:

"Entreat me not to leave thee, and to return from following after thee; for whither thou goest, I will go; and where thou lodgest, I will lodge; thy people shall be my

32

people; and thy God my God; where thou diest, will I die, and there will I be buried: the Lord do so to me, and more also, if aught but death part thee and me."

Ruth was not particularly religious. She said "thy God shall be my God" with no more feeling than "where thou lodgest will I lodge." If she moved she supposed she had to change gods, for gods at that time belonged to the soil, and the change did not affect her deeply. If devotion to Naomi involved devotion to Jehovah, she was prepared to give it, not that she cared for Him, but she did care for Naomi. Jehovah or Chemosh, the god of Moab—it mattered little to her which divinity she worshiped. Religion was merely part of her family obligation and Jehovah was thrown in with her mother-in-law. Ruth was not much in faith; but she was great in faithfulness. And her fidelity to duty brought her among God's people, where she, too, afterwards found a husband and a home, and a lasting name as an ancestress of kings and of Jesus the Christ.

Rahab the believing and Ruth the faithful—how unlike these women are! One hesitates to mention Ruth, whom one associates with the pure air and pleasant sights of country fields and the tender associations of domestic life, in the same breath with the jaded habitué of Jericho's underworld. Ruth had known life's sharpest sorrow—childless widowhood, and more than once with that much-afflicted family of exiles she had walked in the valley of the shadow of death. She is "old in grief and very wise in tears," but her spirit has the buoyancy and courage of youth. Rahab's soul is scarred and embittered.

Rahab is far the cleverer of the two. She is shrewd and resourceful, well able to shift for herself and haggle over her bargains. Ruth, despite her determination, seems a child still, without initiative, looking to Naomi to plan for her and obediently doing what she is told.

But the interesting contrast between the two women is their difference in religious experience. Rahab moves through faith to faithfulness, Ruth through faithfulness to faith. Rahab passes through religion to morality, Ruth through morality to religion. Rahab travels by a sense of her connection with the Unseen into a sense of her obligations to the seen; Ruth travels by a sense of duty to lives at hand into a sense of connection with the mystery of God. Rahab has a maximum of belief with a minimum of conscience, and Ruth a maximum of conscience with a minimum of belief, Rahab begins with an instinct for an invisible Power, Ruth with an instinct for a visible responsibility. Both end at the same point. It takes some time for them to arrive, but we leave them both living full-rounded lives of faith and faithfulness, dutiful wives and loyal believers in God. But they entered the kingdom through opposite doors.

Both types are with us still. There are men who have gone under morally, products partly of the evil conditions of our modern Jerichos and partly of their own feeble wills, with consciences all out of order, but with a mystic sense for unseen Reality, wistfully craving God to rescue them and bring healing and peace. And that faith works. It does not change them completely in an instant. They still show regrettable want of character; but their faith has linked them with a redeeming God, and the process of moral repair and renewal has begun, and will not stop until they are full-grown sons of God.

Again there are the capable and unselfish, products partly of kindlier circumstances and partly of their own creditable well-doing, whose consciences work regularly, and who are without apparent longing for fellowship with a Companion above man. To them religion, if it comes at all, is incidental to their discharge of duty. They may find God necessary to give meaning to their moral universe, or they may find Him a Partner indispensable to

their plans for those they love. He seems to mean little at first, but as they scale the heights of dutifulness they come out on those shining table-lands to which God is moon and sun.

God is far more real to the Rahabs. They have consciously experienced His power. They know that to them in their desperation, gripped by passions that carried them away and downed by overmastering forces of evil all about them, an invisible and most mighty Deliverer came. They passed from darkness to light, from the life where a harlot-producing Jericho claimed them as her own and doomed them to be her wretched products, to a life where old things were put away and love became possible and natural. God is the most obvious Fact in their universe. By faith Rahab the harlot becomes Rahab the wife and mother and an honored figure in Israel.

The Ruths live with God unconsciously. They think about Him no more than of the air they breathe.

> There are who ask not if Thine eye
> Be on them; who in love and truth,
> Where no misgiving is, rely
> Upon the genial sense of youth:
> Glad hearts! without reproach or blot
> Who do Thy work and know it not.

The Rahabs come to God with a more selfish plea than the Ruths. Life for them is full of fearsome forces. They and theirs dwell in a city of destruction. They know the dark and cruel underside of its seemingly gay life. Its society is rotten; they feel that it cannot endure. They want to be rescued. Their favorite hymns are

> Rock of Ages, cleft for me,
> Let me hide myself in Thee;

and

> Jesus, Lover of my soul,
> Let me to Thy bosom fly.

35

The Ruths have no thought of self. They accept God only that they may be more useful to their Naomis. Their favorite hymn is

> O Master, let me walk with Thee
> In lowly paths of service free.

But the selfishness of the Rahabs is no more to be blamed than the unselfishness of the Ruths. Until the Rahabs are reclaimed and transformed by a Power outside themselves, they can be of no service to anybody. They remain a menace. And only as the Ruths consecrate themselves to their Naomis are they of any service to God. God has no preferences. He takes both as He finds them. He lays hold on whatever in them is alive spiritually—on faith in the one and on dutifulness in the other. And He uses it to link them to Himself.

But it is not easy for the Ruths to understand the Rahabs nor for the Rahabs to appreciate the Ruths while both are still only on the way to the full life of the kingdom. The Ruths are likely to define religion in forms which shut out the Rahabs. "I told her," wrote Theodore Parker in a letter to a friend, "there was to my thinking but one religion—that was being good and doing good." "There is only one religion," declared Sir Edward Burne-Jones. "Make the most of your best for the sake of others is the Catholic faith, which except a man believe faithfully he cannot be saved." But to such statements poor outcast Rahab can only answer, "I know that in me dwelleth no good thing." "Who shall deliver me out of the body of this death?"

On the other hand, the Rahabs, with their keen awareness of alliance with Divine Power, are apt to look pityingly on the Ruths as "merely moral" people; or to condemn them as intolerably self-sufficient, because they are burdened with no sense of guilt, and speak perhaps as often of faith in themselves as of faith in God. Someone

called the French linguist and scientist Littré "A saint who did not believe in God." But the Rahabs would not recognize his saintliness and would label him a worldling. The Rahabs are liable to insist that the Ruths make some confession of their own depravity, and declare themselves "born again" before they will admit them as religious. And the Ruths as steadfastly declare that they are religious merely in so far as they are useful, know nothing about being born again, but wish they were more completely what they already are fractionally—conscientious, honorable, kindly servants of men. The Ruths speak of themselves as "the healthy-minded," while to them the Rahabs are the diseased; and the Rahabs retort that the Ruths are unregenerate and need a thoroughgoing conversion before they can be spiritually-minded citizens of the kingdom of heaven.

The shortcomings of the one are irritating to the other. Ruth cannot see for the life of her how Rahab can be a genuine believer in God and still be so selfish, so deceitful, so dishonorable, so heartless. Mr. Gladstone, who certainly prized religion more than most, once wrote:

There is one proposition which the experience of life burns into my soul; it is this, that a man should beware of letting his religion spoil his morality. In a thousand ways, some great, some small, but all subtle, we are daily tempted to that great sin.

And Mr. Huxley declared:

I have never found in people thoroughly imbued with pietism the same notions of honor and straightforwardness that obtain among men of the world.

The Ruths despise the celestial intimacies of the Rahabs because they do not at once render them socially-minded. And Rahab cannot see for the life of her how Ruth can speak so lightly of God, and put no more emphasis on

professing loyalty to Jehovah than she does on moving from Moab to Judah. Each scandalizes the other. The Ruths label the Rahabs hypocrites, and the Rahabs declare that the Ruths are godless. But both are here on the pages of the Bible among the saints and in this list of those from whom the Son of God traces His human descent.

Each has relative advantages. The Ruths are far more loyal friends and reliable citizens; but it is the Rahabs who are the race's seers and bring eternal forces to play amid earthly conditions, even if they show very disagreeable earthly characteristics in the process of bringing them.

Each has peculiar temptations. The Rahabs are in danger of being so occupied with God that they forget men, and love so intensely the Father whom they have not seen that they misuse the brotherhood in the city of Jericho of whom they have seen so much that they have no love for them. The peril of the Ruths lies in fancying that fidelity to their Naomis is the whole of life, and that relations with the Unseen are a mere luxury for those who happen to have a taste for such mystic flights. A Canon of Windsor has told us that his old nurse used to say to him when a child: "If you are a very good little boy, and go to bed without giving trouble, you needn't say your prayers." The Rahabs tend to become inhumanly narrow, the Ruths undivinely flat.

And He who comes of the lineage of both Rahab and Ruth met both in His day. The woman in the city a sinner had insight to see in this Teacher, seated at Simon the Pharisee's table, a friendliness and a life-giving power; and Jesus, because she loved much, bade her "Go in peace," assuring her that her sins were forgiven, for He believed that her love would develop to include even a Simon the Pharisee. The Syro-Phœnician woman comes to Him, with a plea for her little girl, and He grants her request, first holding her off until she waits long enough

to become acquainted with Him, and so open-minded to God. He meets the Rahabs with His welcoming friendship for sinners, with His particular interest in those who know themselves lost. He meets the Ruths, saying "One thing thou lackest," and forces them to a more difficult conscientiousness until in following Him they find an ideal beyond their attainment and cry out for a Father's comradeship. Both Rahab and Ruth find the God they need in Him—Rahab a Saviour who can make her over, Ruth a Fellow-worker who does with her more than she can ask or think for those she so faithfully serves.

Both types are here this morning. Some of us are stronger in faith than in faithfulness, and others in faithfulness than in faith. God does not criticize our weaknesses, but lays hold on our strengths. If we believe in Him, however selfish and weak and soiled we are—believe in Him enough to throw in our lot with His cause, He knows that the alliance with Him will lift us out of our selfishness and rottenness into a love like His own. If we are faithful to our obligations, however little belief we have in God, our loyalty to those He gives us will inevitably draw us into alliance with Him. "Inasmuch as ye have done it unto the least of these My brethren, ye have done it unto Me."

And both Rahab and Ruth exist in the composite nature of each one of us. We live in a Jericho where men prostitute God-given capacities to base uses, where we traitorously forget our obligations to the whole population of Jericho, and live inhumanly careless of what befalls the mass of Jerichoites provided we and ours escape discomfort and disaster. Most of us, like Rahab, are menaces in one form or other to the lives about us, degrading their idealism, and lowering the standards of genuine goodness. Let us lift up our eyes. Invading our world, and more and more subduing it, are forces which advance under a Mightier than Jericho knows—the forces of the Spirit

of Christ. Empowering them is the Lord of heaven and earth. Do we believe that? Can we see in the Spirit of Jesus the supreme Power in the universe? Well, then conspire with Him. In that alliance we shall find ourselves new creatures, and a new life lies before us.

Or, like Ruth, we want to fulfill our social obligations. (Here is Naomi—and who has not several dozen Naomis, and most of them far more difficult and trying than this considerate and affectionate old woman—Naomis who look to us for support, for sympathy, for almost everything.) We wish to be faithful kinsmen, true friends, loyal citizens. *Wishing* is not enough; we must *will* it with the determination of Ruth. She was "steadfastly minded" as Naomi saw. And we shall not possess the power to keep steadfastly-minded save as we say with her of each life we serve "thy God shall be my God." When with Ruth's greater Son we see our Father giving Himself unto the uttermost to discharge His responsibilities to every life He has made, and become His comrades, spending and being spent in the measure of Calvary, we are sufficient for our duties in the fullness of His love.

V

AN APPALLING ALTERNATIVE

"Unless I had believed to see the goodness of the Lord in the land of living—"—Psalm 27:13.

THIS is an incomplete sentence in the Hebrew original: "Ah, had I not believed to see the goodness of the Lord in the land of the living, I—!" We are left to imagine the conclusion. Probably the poet could find no expression strong enough to express his plight under such appalling circumstances. Our translators have supplied "I had fainted." But that is inadequate. If we faint, we come to again; but suppose we must permanently give up the hope of seeing the goodness of the Lord in the land of the living, what then?

What *meaning* remains in life? We look back across long millions of years and read the history of our planet as it has been spelled out for us from the rocks—ages when the crust of the earth was cooling off, ages of ice, plants and creatures battling for a foothold, struggling to keep alive and to continue their kind, ever adapting themselves and changing and at length coming up to man. And then the story—a brief episode of thousands of years against this background of millions—the story of man's career, with his hate and greed and beastliness, with his creative thought and outgoing love, his disquieting conscience and upreaching faith and hope—his Calibans, his Iscariots, his Borgias, his Socrates, his Shakespeare, his Christ. We look ahead and the episode closes. Our planet has run through its cycle and is as dead as the moon.

Man and all his struggles and achievements pass into oblivion; they are a tale that is told but with none to listen to it. And the universe grinds on its unmeaning course.

And as for you and me with our fleeting three score years and ten—a mere wink in the process of the suns—what do we signify? What sense is there in our ideals? What sanctity in our affections? What worth in the standards of honor for which men sacrifice and hazard their necks and spill their blood? Our ideals—will-o'-the-wisps! Our affections—animals huddling together for warmth in the biting cosmic weather! Our standards of honor—auto-suggestions with which the race fools itself to endure and persist! What head or tail will you make out of the comedy and tragedy of our existence?

To those who stop to think, life is a puzzle. Take it at its best, it is a procession in which generation after generation are born, are trained, play their brief rôles, grow weak and outworn and slip away into silence. Take it at its average, and it is not even a well-ordered procession: only part of a generation grows up; only part of that part is capable of learning anything; and only part of that part again does anything with what it has learned. And all along the procession is terribly confused. Some with manifest capacities have no chance to develop them; accident, sickness, calamity continually overtake and break up the ranks; a huge blunder like the world war, almost wipes out the most promising files. And in any case, whither is this procession moving, or what is it doing as it passes on its way? Suppose we are a procession of scholars, trying to learn, but with nothing really worth learning in an irrational universe. We pick up information about the earth we live in, and about predecessors and contemporaries, and acquire the knack of making ourselves a little more comfortable or more dangerous or more destructive, while we live; but what is there to find out and know, if life itself has no reason,

no purpose, no plan in it? A God, above all a good God, is at least a clue suggesting a possible explanation of what is else a blank bewilderment.

Blot God and His goodness out, and what *incentive* to aspiring and unselfish endeavor remains? We take it for granted that it is worth while to protect and prolong human life and to increase man's powers. All our effort in science, in government, in industry, in practical help-fulness, rests on that assumption. But if life have no meaning, of what use is it to add to its years? When we increase man's powers, of what value are they? We can listen in on Europe now over the radio, but what do we hear? Music with its strange power of expressing the unutterable and leading us to the verge of infinity with our aches and our longings and our exultations; songs of love and grief and death and hope; chimes which call to prayer and suggest to earth-bound mortals some-thing afar from the sphere of our sorrow. But suppose the music and the songs and the chimes only lead us to an infinite void? Suppose they are at best opiates to dull our senses and stupefy our minds and make pitiless existence a little more tolerable?

And as for our cherished scheme of races living in mutual respect and service, of nations working together in good-will, of the world's work carried on as a sacred ministry by a comradeship of mankind, of childhood safe-guarded from exploitation and given the fullest chance to grow in body and mind and spirit, of youth stimulated and trained to appreciate, to know, to serve, of life down to the grave enriched and ennobled with understanding and sympathy—do we not tacitly assume that this uni-verse of ours favors these desires of our hearts and these dreams of our consciences? Hosts of socially-minded and high-principled men and women in our day are living and toiling for these ends. Many of them have discarded religion and never give a thought to God. He is an

hypothesis for which they tell us that they have no need. Engrossed in improving our earth, it is a matter of indifference to them whether it be "ampler day divinelier lit or homeless night without." But suppose this assumption that our world is favorable to these fraternal and kindly plans be unwarranted, suppose the universe cares as little about our schemes for human well-being as the ocean cares for tiny forts of sand which children build on the beach, suppose a turn of the cosmic tide should sweep them away, leaving no trace behind, what heart have we or they for battling and toiling for a friendly world? And if you take God and His goodness out of the picture—the objects faith supplies—does the face of this universe look friendly and favorable to our hearts' longings or stonily uncaring? Who can gird himself day after day to endure and struggle and toil for the upbuilding of the ideal commonwealth and for the encouragement and ennoblement of men at his side, if there is no assurance that the universe makes possible his hopes, and will not bring them to nothing? "Unless I had believed to see the goodness of the Lord in the land of the living,"

> Black despair—
> The shadow of a starless night were thrown
> Over the world in which I move alone.

And what *hope* is there in those situations where we and all human knowledge and power put together are helpless? Death shadows us and ours. It does not seem unfriendly when it peacefully closes a well-rounded career. But that feeling of its friendliness would vanish did we not assume that the acquired skill and matured character were utilized elsewhere. You recall William James' reply to the query: "Do you believe in a personal immortality?" "Never keenly; but more strongly as I grow older." "Why?" "Because I am just getting fit to live."

44

And when death comes in childhood, or when it comes to young and vigorous folk with the world before them, or when it comes in the noonday of usefulness taking most needed father or mother, husband or wife, leader and inspiration of many, something within us rises in protest. Unless for them there is the goodness of the Lord in the land of the living, "earth is darkness to the core, and dust and ashes all that is."

And in situations where something far worse than death confronts us—moral tragedies, where love has been sinned against, or honor trampled in the mud, or trust betrayed, and a life is wrecked and carries down with it other lives to pain and shame—situations where instinctively the most irreligious exclaim, "O my God!"— if that cry dies away in empty space, if there be no Ear to hear, no Heart to sympathize, no Love to redeem— then can we any better than this ancient Hebrew poet find language to express man's condition? "Unless I had believed to see the goodness of the Lord in the land of the living—!"

We talk so lightly about belief and unbelief; we think a man's creed makes little difference; religion is generally considered a luxury, which one may take if his taste inclines that way, but which he can do quite well without. Apart from faith in God, a good God, a God like Christ, life lacks meaning, lacks zest, lacks hope—yes, and lacks *beauty*.

We live in a lovely earth. There are so many fair and delightful things here, that we blaspheme if we disparage them. Even if there be no second life, we must not run down the goodness of this one. A distinguished British thinker wrote:

We shall not speak of love or of one's daily meals or of science or of Shakespeare; but he who has seen the sea and the blue of heaven, and the moon and the stars, who has clomb a mountain, who has heard a bird

in the woods, who has spoken and been spoken to, who has seen a sock or a shoe of his own child, and has known a mother—he will bow the knee and thank his God and call it good, even though his lot in the end be nothingness.

Yes, but he is thanking his God. The fair sights of sea and stars, the tenderer associations of little children and one's own mother, have a meaning. They are the goodness of the Lord in the land of the living. One can look up through them to a Heart yonder with such grateful confidence as to say: "Though He put me to an endless sleep, yet I will trust in Him." But suppose the beauty of earth and sky, and the love of our homes means nothing, suppose they be by-products and casual incidents in a vast process that has no plan, because there is neither Mind nor Heart nor Conscience behind and in it, what a hideous cheat! What an ugly mockery! And did we not believe to see the goodness of the Lord in the land of the everliving, would not a haunting sense of fateful extinction darken the loveliness of sunlight on the sea and the twinkle of starlight in the evening sky, and make tragically terrible the brief moments when children are children to us, and a mother's love is spared to bless us? Is not the beauty of life largely due to an assumption of "a Light that never was on sea or land"? Was not the singer telling us the secret of finding this life fair, who sang:

> I walk as one who sees the joy shine through
> Of the Other Life behind our life, like the stars
> behind the blue . . . ?

Well, granted that meaning and zest and hope and beauty go when one parts with the vision of the goodness of the Lord in the land of the living, suppose one cannot see it, must one not honestly face facts? Certainly. But let us be sure that we face all the facts. It is common

to concentrate on the harsh and disagreeable and menacing elements and write a lamentation. What of redemptive factors which postpone or prevent or retrieve the expected disaster?

We look out of our windows some winter mornings on a city shrouded in a murky pall. It is amazingly dark: the unseasonable warmth, the fog, the smoke, make a dense atmosphere, but it is not night. There is something struggling in the murk. We have no glimpse of the sun, none of that gleam and glitter which we associate with a snappy midwinter dawn; but the sun's rays are at work, and we are aware of their presence. We know it is not night; something different is there.

Is it not a parable of life? We do not actually see God's goodness in the land of the living. Many have but rare glimpses of it. Earth has a murky spiritual atmosphere. It is easily possible for folk of a certain cast of mind to declare that there is no Sun of righteousness. But the mass of mankind always have felt, and still feel, that we are not living in godless night. There is Something here, "a Presence that will not be put by"; rays of love penetrate the thick selfishness. To many they are not clear enough to lead them to phrase a faith in the Sun—a God of goodness. To many more such a God is an unconscious assumption with whom they never directly concern themselves. But there has always been an elect minority who in the darkest and murkiest day assert their faith in Him. You recall Carlyle's exquisite tribute to his wife: "She was the rainbow to my poor dripping day." To believing folk in every age, God, of whose goodness wives are a supreme sacrament, has been just that—the rainbow to their poor dripping day.

And what is wanted at the hour is a Church throughout the world of Christians who see the rainbow—"the goodness of the Lord in the land of the living" *"See"* it—another psalmist adds one more of our senses: "O taste

and see that the Lord is good." What is wanted is a Church of believing men and women who have experienced, who have tasted and who feed on the goodness of God, and say with assurance: "We know: He is meat and drink to us, our life."

Have you happened on a sonnet by a minor poetess entitled, "The Travel Bureau"?

All day she sits behind a bright brass rail
Planning proud journeyings in terms that bring
Far places near—high-colored words that sing—
"The Taj-Mahal at Agra" . . . "Kashmir's vale" . . .
Spanning wide spaces with her clear detail,
  "Seville or Fiesole in spring"
"Thro' the Fjords in June"—her words take wing:
She is the minstrel of the great Out-Trail.

At half-past five she puts her maps away,
Pins on a gray, meek hat and braves the sleet,
A timid eye on traffic. Dully gray
The house that harbors her in a gray street,
The close, sequestered, colorless retreat
Where she was born; where she will always stay.

Whenever a Christian congregation meets and listens to the great words of the Bible, enshrining experiences of men of old with God, experiences renewed again and again through the centuries; whenever a congregation joins in psalm and hymn—minstrels of the great Up-Trail —and bows in the mystery of prayer while thoughts travel forth to the Infinite, we are telling one another, and telling the world of secret places of the Spirit, richer in inspiration than towns or buildings where man's most momentous happenings have occurred and fairer in beauty than the loveliest spots on earth. We are a travel bureau to one another, suggesting journeys of the soul to places of refreshment and comfort and healing, and to mountain peaks of far-sweeping vision. But what if the dwell-

ing-places of our own spirits be gray, colorless retreats, unvisited by any gleam of the Divine Presence? What if the goodness of the Lord be a mere phrase on our lips, and every experience of these friends of God as much a hearsay as the sights of India and Italy to the woman at the London desk?

There are peaks of vision whence God lets us see what He wills for us. Have we climbed them and looked at our life with God? There is holy ground where a man kneels and commits his way to a wiser Guide, and finds his paths directed. Do we know His leading? There is a fountain for sin and for uncleanness, and the hosts of the redeemed have visited it, and come away born anew. Have we taken the soil and stain of life and the weakness and disease of our own wills to it for cleansing? There is a place of power to which ordinary folk have gone, and come away to do extraordinary things. Have we ever sought this reinforcement? There is a spring of living water, of which tired and disheartened men and women drink and lift up their heads in courage and indomitable hope. There are outlooks whence the eyes of the heart have sight of the splendor of a diviner day, and where the beauty of the Lord comes upon and transfigures wistful spirits, and ever after their faces are "lit with their loving and aglow with God." This—and we have not begun to circle the spiritual globe or to map out the travels of the soul and its amazing discoveries—this is the goodness of the Lord in the land of the living. It is exhaustlessly rich, as each generation bears witness, and it invariably suggests other and fairer goals of our journeying where "eye hath not seen, nor ear heard, nor hath it entered into the heart of man to conceive the things which God hath prepared for them that love Him." But only those who taste and see are sure, and can make others want to taste and see.

Readers of Dr. George A. Gordon's autobiographical

volume must have noticed the letter Mrs. William James wrote him, when she asked him to conduct the funeral service for her husband:

I want you to officiate at the funeral as one of William's friends, and also as a man of faith. That is what he was; I want no hesitation or diluted utterance at William's funeral.

An old eighteenth century Scottish divine, a man of deep personal devoutness, Thomas Halyburton, said to the physician who was attending him in his last illness: "There is a reality in religion, Doctor, but this is an age that hath lost the sense of it." Ours is an age that feels for and craves the sense of it. Thoughtful folk have been faced with the alternative: "Unless I believe to see the goodness of the Lord in the land of the living—" and the alternative makes us shudder. But the goodness of the Lord is real only to those who venture upon it utterly, use it as the clue to life, the stimulus to serve, the stay on which they rest in tranquil confidence.

"The goodness of the Lord"—is the phrase too vague? See it in the face of Jesus Christ—yes, see it in His pierced hands and feet and side. He is part of our world, an ever-increasing part of it, as living a force and a more living force than any most alive in the land of the living. There are flashes of the Christlike all about us, beams of His Spirit penetrating many a sphere where He is unknown by name, rays of His ideal piercing through the most sordid real.

> Its lovely gleamings
>   Seemings show
> Of things not seemings.
>   And I gaze,
> Knowing that beyond my ways
>   Verily
> All these *are*.

VI

THE REALISM OF FAITH

"For he that hath, to him shall be given: and he that hath not, from him shall be taken even that which he hath."
—Mark 4:25.

IF WE stumbled on this saying for the first time, and were asked to guess who said it, would we attribute it to Jesus of Nazareth? It sounds so differently from the Beatitudes—"Blessed are the poor in spirit, the meek, the merciful, they that mourn"—and from the Golden Rule. It seems incompatible with Him whose chief concern were the least, the last, the lost. It rings like the slogan of a buccaneering acquisitive society. One might assign it to a Roman thinker rationalizing imperialism; but hardly to the Figure who laid down His life at Calvary. If the Biblical flavor of its English led us to conjecture a scriptural author, we might fancy it a maxim of the worldly-wise Book of Proverbs, akin to "the rich man's wealth is his strong city; the destruction of the poor is their poverty." Many of the Proverbs seem a long way from the mind of Jesus, but no farther from it than this saying.

Have we an accurate view of Jesus? He is a shrewd realist telling us what life *is*. We imagine that He discourses only on what He would have it be. But He starts with the world as He finds it, and believes that the basic structure of life is God's handiwork. He observes that the sun shines on the evil and the good, and that rains fall on just and unjust. We are disposed to object that

51

this is both unfair and undesirable. It is discouraging to the just and not disciplinary to the unjust. How correcting it would be if the sun underwent a total eclipse immediately over the acres of the farmer who watered his milk, and marketed his peaches with the large ripe fruit on top of the basket and worm-eaten runts underneath, while its rays streamed benignly down on the meadows of his honest neighbor! Most of us have a number of improvements to suggest in the arrangements of our planet; but Jesus accepted sun and rain as they are, and read from them something of the character of the large-hearted Lord of life. In this saying He states an abiding impression which life has made on Him. "He that hath, to him is given: from him that hath not is taken even that which he hath."

Whether or not we think this is as it should be, let us begin by noticing that so it is. He that hath *health*, to him is given. Food in plenty nourishes him, exercise invigorates him, wind and sunshine and rain agree with and brace him, stiff work calls out his energy and he rises to the occasion. He that hath not health finds the food which he likes indigestible, exercise a strain on heart or lungs, sunshine hurting his eyes and causing a headache, damp weather laying him low in misery, and the mere prospect of strenuous labor brings on a nervous collapse.

He that hath *intelligence*, to him books, travel, knotty problems, the welter of ideas which flood in from a stimulating community, all the happenings which befall him, contribute knowledge. He that hath not intelligence, to him books are dull, travel bewildering, problems upsetting, the welter of contemporary life confusing, and everything that overtakes him adds to the muddle of his inexpertness.

To him that hath *appreciation* literature in prose and verse opens its treasures, music leads him off into satisfactions beyond telling, nature in the amplitude of a

mountain outlook or in the sublimity of the sky at the end of city streets feeds his soul, art in lines or colors delights his eye, and folk—folk of all sorts—have interest and meaning. To the unappreciative these scarcely exist: literature bores him, music sends him to sleep or is a painful interruption to his chatter, nature is unnoticed, art belongs in the museums which, he thanks God, he does not have to visit, and people—well, he may say with David Harum a generation ago that the more he sees of them, the more he prefers dogs.

To him that hath *conscience* any place where he happens to live brings responsibilities, any community in which he finds himself opens doors for service, any task which he undertakes is a duty to be discharged, any new acquaintance is an added loyalty and a summons to sympathy, marriage and family lifelong obligations which claim him for better, for worse. He that lacks conscience, to him any place affords chances to go wrong, any community supplies associates who assist him to fritter away his time or to waste himself more disastrously, any task laid on him an opportunity to see with how small an output of effort he can get by, any new acquaintance one more person to be used, marriage and family tragic possibilities of wrecking other lives by selfishness or of abusing the love lavished on him to puff his egotism. From him that hath not, life, like a sinister magnet, pulls whatever might build character.

To him that hath *faith* doubts open windows to larger thoughts of God, strains develop trust, black midnights sharpen the eyes of his heart to see God where He is most invisible, ordeals discover for him unsuspected divine resources, those "rubs, doublings and wrenches" of which Sir Thomas Browne spoke, "which pass a while under the effects of chance" prove the guiding hand of God, and even abysses where he feels utterly God-forsaken turn out in retrospect holy places where underneath him

were the everlasting arms. To him that hath not faith, doubts destroy the beliefs with which he was equipped in youth, difficulties harden his unbelief, depressions convince him that talk of Providence is nonsense, successes bolster his self-sufficiency, failures make him curse his luck, sorrows leave him embittered and cynical. "He that hath not, from him shall be taken even that which he hath."

We said that Jesus accepted life as it is, looked steadily at it with penetrating eyes, and read from it the character of God. Religion is often derided as "wishful thinking." Finding life grim, men fly off to a fancied world patterned to their heart's desire—

> a shadow isle of bliss
> 'Midmost the beating of the steely sea.

But is there any "wishful thinking" in such a statement as this? What more honest facing and frank reporting of fact can you ask? Jesus is interpreting a principle of the Kingdom of Heaven; He is confronting us with God's ways in an earth which He controls. Jesus calls God Father; He believes that God is love. But notice the effects of love on him that hath and on him that hath not.

The sunshine filters down so softly through the atmosphere in our temperate zone, confers such countless benefits on vegetation and living creatures, and so enhances the loveliness of countryside or city street, that we do not quarrel with Wordsworth's metaphor in the "Prelude" —"*hurtless* light." If we witness an eclipse, it startles us to see the jagged, shooting jets of flame at the moment of totality which disclose the fiery planet the sun is. Of course if we stop to think about it, the genial rays that stream down on us are as destructive to some things as they are vitalizing to others. The sun would have no "healing in its wings" (to use a prophet's phrase) were it not deadly to certain bacilli.

54

THE REALISM OF FAITH

"The Sun of righteousness," as this same prophet calls God, both creates and destroys. God is love always and everywhere, and therefore to the unloving and unlovely a consuming fire.

Eclipses in the life of mankind which darken a world in gloom seem proof to some that ours is a godless universe. But eclipses of the sun are revealing occurrences when scientists gather to enlarge their knowledge of that mysterious planet which plays so momentous a rôle in the life of our globe.

Are we not passing through just such a revelation of God, who is Light? From nations and communities that have not certain moral qualities—conscience to consider the distribution of wealth as attentively as its acquisition, conscience to view technological improvements in industry in their effects on workers, conscience to include all nations as well as our own in the fellowship of enjoyment—from them is taken that material security of which they were boastfully sure. And to those with wakening consciences, who will estimate how much is being given? In the after-look of history our generation may prove a revealing period when the Sun of righteousness rose with healing in His wings and some of the world's sorest ills were done away—self-centered nationalism, ruthless competition, neglect of the human beings who create wealth, above all neglect of the spirit of brotherhood in industry, in politics, in international relations. Yes, a creative period when spiritual riches came into being. "To him that hath shall be given."

In our Gospels this saying of Christ's is recorded in two connections. Once when He is justifying His use of parables, and warning "Take heed what ye hear." Such stories as He told about four kinds of soil on which a sower dropped his seed may be merely interesting anecdotes or they may transmit a message which alters a man's life.

What numerous voices are speaking to us through events and friends and books and teachers and the trends of a day dizzying with change! For what have we ears? The atmosphere about us, as we know from our radio sets, is full of sounds. We cannot listen to all of them at once—very fortunately, for together they are a confused jangle. We select. We tune in with a receiver for a specified wave-length. Our interest is decisive in keying attention and determining to what we listen. In the same church, the same business community, the same cultural environment, two men will hear utterly different things. To him that hath ears for the voice of the Spirit, the wisdom of God will speak, and life will glow with divine purpose. To him that hath not, there will come a jumble of sounds leaving him bewildered. "Take heed what ye hear."

The saying occurs again in the parable of the servants whose master gave them money to trade with. Luke has all three receiving a pound apiece; Matthew gives one man five talents, a second two and a third one. The point is not what each starts with but how he uses it. The intolerable fault is unprofitableness. The servant who is afraid of losing, and therefore does nothing with his pound, has it taken from him and it is given to the servant who can do most with it.

It is a chief peril of contemporary life that we become observers and critics of affairs rather than actors in them. We discuss faith instead of employing it in achievements for God. We appraise the movements of the day instead of flinging ourselves into the enterprise of making a juster world. We assess Christ instead of letting Him rule our minds and search our consciences and use us. There must be rigorously critical thinking. No intelligent person dare leave his judgment behind. But here are gifts of knowledge, of conscience, of faith—the supreme gift of Christ—not to be thought about and discussed. They are trusts

committed to us with which to bring returns to God. The one unpardonable defect in a trustee is no income. "Take therefore the talent from him."

Again and again one sees that happen. A distinguished professor at Yale University in the last generation came on the faculty an active Christian, a clergyman, but as the years passed he seemed to lose all religious interest and was rated among the uncaring. He once said:

"I never consciously gave up a religious belief. It was as if I had put my beliefs into a drawer, and when I opened it, there was nothing there at all."

From him that useth not is taken.

But with this stark realism, open-eyed to what life *is*, how magnificently hopeful Jesus remains: "Unto everyone that hath shall be given, and he shall have abundance," one version of His saying reads. This is the basis of His sublime confidence in some who had just a little. And surely we find ourselves typified in them.

There were the wistful—looking for a diviner day in the earth when stupidities and injustices should cease. There were Jesus' first followers whose consciences had been roused by John. How cordially Jesus welcomed them, kept them with Him, and in some months' time enabled them to grow into men who changed the world. To him that hath this divine discontent inestimably much is given.

There were the restive with themselves. Recall that wild and debased brigand hung up beside Jesus at Golgatha with enough longing to be different to ask: "Lord, remember me." If we really wish to be other than we have been, to be rid of laziness, conceit, self-coddling, thoughtlessness, and will to be hard-working, humble, disciplined, considerate, and turn to Christ wistfully, there is no question of a substantial result "Today shalt thou be with Me." In His company our will to become

like Him is incalculably reinforced. To him that hath is given and he has abundance.

There was the wavering disciple, whose record so resembles ours of whom our acquaintance say: "He a Christian? yes, but look at this in his thinking, and this in his manner of life, and this other in his treatment of people." We ourselves are uncomfortable in our disloyalty. An hour when the figure of Christ is set before us again does not make us less so. He has a mysterious faculty of dealing personally with us: "Lovest thou Me?" "Lord," and we are sincere in saying it, "Lord, Thou knowest all things" (a sad mess most of them) "Thou knowest that I love Thee." That to Him is all important; the rest He brushes aside. Unto Him that hath persisting loyalty, however marred, is given. "Feed my sheep." We may have next to nothing to share, but sharing works an inevitable miracle. "With what measure ye mete, it shall be measured unto you, *and more shall be given you.*" Never forget that divine supplement.

There was that attached but despondent disciple, Thomas. And he is the counterpart of thousands of contemporary Christians. We know that we could not part altogether with Christ, if we tried. He has woven Himself inextricably into our affections. But as we look about we cannot see that His cause is markedly gaining. In many particulars it seems to be slipping. We are tempted to think ourselves bound to a forlorn hope and followers of a spent and defeated Master. Well, our impressions, be they sanguine or pessimistic, are not of first importance. They vary with temperament and a man's immediate circumstances; and the field is so vast, the issues at any moment in history so complex, that an individual's judgment of how the battle is going has little worth. What alone counts is attachment to Christ, the resolve to bear Him company, be He succeeding or failing: "Let us also go, that we may die *with Him.*" It happened that, after

Thomas said that, he witnessed not a disaster but a wonderful achievement, and knew Christ the Life-giver. But Thomas would never have had part in that and in many another victory, unless he had had, along with his misgivings, steadfast personal devotion to Christ. To him that hath this—whatever else he lack—is given, and he shares in the life-bringing triumphs of his Lord.

VII

ABOVE ALL THAT WE THINK

"But the lad knew not anything."—I Sam. 20:39.

AND the lad was none the poorer for not knowing. Why
should his young mind be defiled with knowledge of a
half-insane and jealous king's foul plan to murder his
once-loved musician and warrior?

There are many times when one looks enviously at
children happily unconscious of life's tragedies. Their
simpler world cannot find place for them. They live in
the immediate present, absorbed in things which they see
or do. This lad was keenly interested when Jonathan
took him with him on an expedition. He watched eagerly
as Jonathan drew his bow, and he found it a thrilling
game to run and find and bring back the arrows. It never
entered his head that Jonathan's calls to him had an
ulterior meaning. Children are born trustful, and a lad
accustomed to the company of a lovable man like Jonathan would have no occasion to have his trust shaken.
Why should he suspect that Jonathan was using him as
a factor in a plot to escape murder? "But the lad knew
not anything."

It is this preoccupation with what is going on in their
world and their oblivion of things bitterly hard for us
which render children such comforts to older folk. Lonely
men and women in their sorrows escape from themselves
by living with a child and entering into his fresh interest in simple happenings. Tired minds come home from
a day of problems and cares to romp in a nursery for

a half hour or to listen to a child's ardent account of his day's doings and be recreated. There are few sights more beautiful than that of some gray head, over which life's waves have rolled, recovering zest and losing poignant memories in play with a child. Thank God for constantly remaking this children's world—a world of bows and arrows, of scampering and finding, of delight in being with someone who is respected and loved and sharing what he is doing—a world without suspicions, where words mean what they sound and no more, where there is no foreboding of danger and pain and death and parting.

And yet what an immeasurably poorer world we should live in if the things we do did not possess a hidden meaning! Every action of the lad that day had results of which he was unaware. His attention to Jonathan's archery and his swift pursuit of the arrows were training his eyes and muscles; but he never thought of that. His comradeship with Jonathan, little as he suspected what was uppermost in Jonathan's mind, was preparing him to be a friend; and he never thought of that. This is life's method of unconscious education. And David and Jonathan knew as little as the lad what they were doing. David was trying to discover the obsessions of a madman and trying to protect himself against his machinations; Jonathan was loyally helping a friend in peril. But David running off to live as a precarious fugitive did not foresee himself a king, and certainly did not forefancy that his kingship was to become the symbol of a nation's ideal, to be some day fulfilled in a Figure adored by millions. Jonathan could not have guessed that he was making himself the type of perfect friendship for generations unborn, and enabling God to set on Saul's throne in his place another whose descendant was to be the Friend of mankind. Of all this they knew not anything.

Everything that we are and do has a meaning beyond itself. There is always a much bigger world about us,

of which our conscious world is only a tiny fraction. We are engrossed in an archer and his arrows, or in our friend and his danger, or in a lunatic of whose delusion we are the innocent victim; but this is not the whole of life. It is a tiny segment of a much vaster world. Jonathan's and David's world included a great deal more than the lad's world; and of their world of fears and loyalties and hopes the lad knew nothing. And round about Jonathan's and David's world was the still larger world of God's purposes, of which they knew even less than the lad knew of their thoughts and plans. You remember Matthew Arnold's lines:

> As chartered by some unknown Powers
> We stem across the sea of life by night.

But are we entirely sure that the lad knew not anything? It is not quite so easy to conceal one's thoughts from a child. He may not know of what you are thinking, but his intuition gives him an inkling of something on your mind. Probably there was a serious air about Jonathan's shooting that day by the stone Ezel, and an emphasis in the tones of his call: "Is not the arrow beyond thee? Make speed, haste, stay not," which gave the boy an uncanny feeling. Something surely was afoot, though just what he did not know.

And from earliest times, doubtless millions of years ago, man has felt that life suggested something beyond itself. Nature in sky and tree and rock, life with its mysteries of birth and growth and decay and death, his own experiences of love and joy and pain and sorrow, hinted at profounder significances. He found himself in a world of many meanings but of no clear speech. Objects, occurrences, his own heart and conscience, inferred more than they said. They seemed to signify something, and he tried to make out what it was. At times he felt that he succeeded. He arrived at interpretations of the world and

life and death; but there were always overtones or undertones beyond his capacity to catch and understand. He lived in a haunted universe. There was a presence here not to be put by. His thoughts were constantly being carried beyond the things he saw and did to question what they meant? what were they doing to him and his? what was life for? what was back of it? what or who controlled it? and what was this mysterious It or He doing? "The lad knew not anything," but he surmised something.

And for all the startling advances in knowledge life remains just as mysterious to us as to a caveman. It is wholesome for us to sit down with some really competent scientist and let him bring us up to date in what has been discovered in our universe. And from such a survey one comes convinced of this: that nothing is what it seems. We think of matter as solid; but that is just what it is not. We place our feet on the floor and fancy that we are standing on something substantial. To a physicist it is as though we had set our feet on a swarm of flies—a seething mass of centers of energy. We fancy that we are standing on a steady earth and holding our heads erect towards the fixed stars: in reality we are hanging on by our feet to a whirling globe, which is traveling at high velocity amid myriads of similarly rotating planets. We talk about an empty space, but as we put our hand out into it our scientist sees the atmosphere pressing with a force of fourteen pounds on every square inch of our body. And if our common-sense view of such things as the floor beneath us and the space about us needs constant revision, should we be surprised that all our guesses at the remoter meanings of existence are just children's surmises? But that is not to say that hidden meanings are not really there. Professor Eddington concluded his series of Gifford Lectures on "The Nature of the Physical World" with the statement:

My own concern lest I should have been talking nonsense ends in persuading me that I have to reckon with something that could not possibly be found in the physical world.

The lad knew not anything, but instinctively felt in the situation something beyond him.

And was this lad so hopelessly ignorant that day by the stone Ezel? He knew Jonathan; he was his companion; he shared so far as he could Jonathan's plans. Indeed, Jonathan needed him to carry them out. Jonathan had concerns that he could not tell him; but he was an essential factor in fulfilling Jonathan's friendly purpose. The lad trusted this loyal man, and he did what he was told to do. Perhaps he found out years later what was transpiring that memorable day when David escaped with his life. Perhaps the lad never knew this side the grave the part he had played in effecting the flight of Israel's future king. Whether he ever knew or not is unimportant. The point is that his devotion to Jonathan gave him a part in a larger world than his own boyish world, connected him with purposes beyond his capacity to understand at the time, and enabled him to fulfill a rôle in plans immeasurably significant not only for his nation but for mankind. He knew not anything in the hidden realm of politics, but he knew and obeyed one who belonged in a realm more profound than his.

And it was so too with Jonathan. The madly jealous Saul had tried to convince him that David was a menace to his future as well as to the king's; but Jonathan was faithful to the highest that he knew—to the sacred obligations of friendship. He risked his life for his friend. Of David's future, and of the larger future to which to all time David's figure is related, he had no glimpse. His appreciation of David may have made him sense that he was not a common man, but possessed unusual gifts

that would carry him far. But that was not the issue. David was his friend, and in loyalty he was bound to warn him of his peril and aid him to escape. And that loyalty of Jonathan to his highest linked him with a larger world than that in which he lived, connected him with purposes beyond his understanding, and enabled him to play a decisive part in a plan whose ultimate bearings even you and I cannot as yet descry.

And does not this bring us to the very essence of religion? Through a myriad hints, man has come to find himself in a haunted universe. Things about him and within him have inferences. He cannot get away from the feeling of Something or Someone unseen to whom they point. More sensitive spirits have dimly discerned what and who this mysterious Soul of the universe is. Some have been very sure of it and in that faith have been able to achieve singular triumphs. One in particular has seemed to be God's intimate—to understand Him more clearly, to share His purpose more fully, to be more congenial with Him than any other.

And what Jesus was and remains casts a spell over us. We cannot say that we understand God, that we know what He is doing with us and ours, that we know His ways in this baffling world. But Jesus we know. This Man of Nazareth and Calvary draws us to Himself with an irresistible friendliness. He will not call us servants, but friends, and He wishes us to share all His secrets. We cannot; but that is not His fault. We are spiritually too immature. But He draws us into His companionship, and we find ourselves in our childish way entering into His faith and saying "Our Father," becoming comrades of His purpose and seeking to bring about the reign of that Father's love in our earth, entering into His hope that such love shall rule both here and in all the mansions of the Father's eternal home, catching Jesus' Spirit and trying to think and act with His mind. Through Him we

feel ourselves linked with a vaster world than we can understand, connected with purposes that sweep in orbits far beyond our thought, made partners in momentous business where the relatively small things which we do from day to day—mere hunting and fetching of arrows—have eternal significance. He is our Jonathan—and one can scarcely resist commenting on the meaning of that Hebrew name "God's gift"—a friendly Man, the one spiritual Adult in a world of children, who admits us to His comradeship, who bids us do certain things—seemingly small and unimportant as they are against the cosmic background—but things through which we share the purpose of Him who is Lord of earth and heaven. Though still mere lads, knowing next to nothing and sometimes literally nothing of the ultimate meaning of what we do, we are used in the far-reaching plans of God.

This conception of two worlds—the immediate world of our knowledge and the larger inclusive world of God's purposes—helps us to interpret our experiences. Our world is a strange jumble of good and evil; it has in it the trust of this lad and the suspicion of Saul, the loyalty of a friend and the half-crazed jealousy of a would-be murderer. Such is our world in which it is often hard to say what is divine and what is diabolic, what is of God's creating and what of man's marring. But connected with our world, and including it in a vaster whole, is this other realm of our faith—the world of our ideals and of God's realities far transcending our ideals. Of this divine world we know scarcely anything, but we believe it to be real. Indeed, without it our world has no meaning.

What is it all but a trouble of ants in the gleam of a million million of suns?

And for us Christians Jesus is the connection between these worlds, the Mediator (as the New Testament calls

Him) between God and man. He is Man in this mixed world of ours, where He meets both trustful folk and murderers who nail Him to a cross. But whether trusted and followed or suspected and crucified, He moved in this larger world of God's will. Instinctively we feel that, even if it puzzles us to make out how He did so. He does for man what Sir William Watson hailed a skylark as doing:

> Thou art native to the spheres,
> And of the courts of heaven art free;
> And carriest to his temporal ears
> News from eternity;
> And lead'st him to the dizzy verge,
> And lur'st him o'er the dazzling line,
> Where mortal and immortal merge,
> And human dies divine.

And for us to cleave to this most friendly Man and to be guided by His mind is to live in our world of mixed human happenings and in this other world where God's will is done, and effects consequences far above out of our sight.

This does not mean that when we follow Christ mystery vanishes from life. How can it while we are still children? It will always be to us an odd world, where things happen queerly. How strange it would have seemed to this lad had he seen David hiding and Jonathan giving him advice through such cryptic words as his calls to him: "The arrow is beyond thee." Yes, and more than an odd world—sometimes a heart-breaking world. Perhaps even the lad sensed something of Jonathan's tragic feeling as he was sending away the friend dear to him as his own soul, and sending him away because a father whom he loved and revered was losing his mind and thirsting for this friend's blood. This lad who knew not anything is a useful reminder of our own immature in-

telligence. We must expect life to be puzzling to us. We must be alert and curious to find out all we can and at the same time accustom ourselves to not knowing. We need not blame God as secretive. Who knows but that His reserve pains Him as much as it does us. Perhaps it pains Him more. He may be "dying to tell" (to employ our vernacular expression) when we are "dying to know." He may long for comrades of His vaster plans, and have to content Himself with half-ignorant children. We have to learn to open wide our minds and push to the farthest end of intelligence, and also to bear without resentment the apparent reticence of God. A lad cannot be told much. He would not understand were he told. And in any case we agree that he is better off without knowing.

But this does not mean that you and I are doomed here in this schoolroom existence to childish lives—far from it. Life is a kindergarten where we learn primary lessons and are educated in elementary things; and life is at the same time a battlefield where even lads hold positions which make them factors for victory or for disaster. Doubtless most of the things we think of and attend to from day to day seem trivial. Running after arrows in a field is a boy's work. It does not seem in the least important. Our day's programs—what are they? what do they signify? Yes, it was a boy's work, but it achieved a man's purpose, and a noble man's purpose—it saved a friend's life. It did more: it accomplished God's providence and eventually helped to save mankind.

Of course not every lad scampering after arrows in a field does that. It all depends on whether or not he is connected with a world of affairs higher than his own. Here was a devoted man, Jonathan, seeking to be true even at the risk of his life to a friend in need; and the lad, obeying him, had his childish doings given momentous meaning. Here in the midst of our race of Lilliputian

ABOVE ALL THAT WE THINK

mortals on this minor planet has come a supreme Friend,
whose fidelity is forever attested by prints of nails in His
hands, and we, very ordinary children of men, by com-
panying with Him and trying to follow His mind in all
our small doings, can be confident that we achieve something too great and too far-reaching for us to compre-
hend—that we carry forward the eternal purpose of our
loving God.

VIII

INSPIRATIONS THAT FAIL

"And it came to pass after a while, that the brook dried up."—I Kings 17:7.

THE editor of the Book of Kings happily found among the materials available for his biography of Elijah not only a record of the public acts of this prophet, but two stories of personal experiences which befell him. These stories take us behind the scenes (so to speak) and show us the man being educated.

The aim of the course was to supply Elijah with a confident dependence on resources outside himself—a lesson by no means easy for any of us to learn, and an education without which none of us is ready for highest service. We never have the courage to shoulder the responsibilities we should, to set our minds to the questions we ought to think through, to brace ourselves to undergo the ordeals that must be faced, to take the risks which must be ventured if we are to be leaders in social advance, until we know how to say in the language of religion: "Our sufficiency is of God."

Our wise Teacher gives His workmen fairly early an introductory course in want—a course like Elijah's experience of famine. We learn that neither we nor anybody else possesses wisdom or ability or conscience or means adequate for the demands of the hour. Then God keeps us provided for under circumstances when we expected to be utterly at a loss, furnishing us from unsuspected sources. We learn how vast are His supplies,

70

and come to believe the statement of one who went through this schooling: "God is able to make all grace abound unto you; that ye, having always all sufficiency in everything, may abound in every good work." You may smile at that sweeping statement of the apostle's, but the man's career is evidence that he knew of what he was speaking.

And along with this education in supplies from beyond our ken, Elijah is given a special course in having his supplies suddenly stop: "It came to pass after a while, that the brook dried up." One can fancy the prophet's anxiety as he watched the trickle of water growing less and less, and his despair when one morning there was none at all—just the parched gravelly bed under a pitiless sun. He had settled down beside that brook believing that God would surely care for him there, and the brook was failing him.

This is a familiar experience. In the midst of a spiritually arid world we discover a stream of inspiration—our Cherith—and gratefully we live beside it and draw on it day after day. Sometimes the brook is a friend who stimulates our mind, quickens our conscience, satisfies our heart. God puts beside us those like brooks by the way, of which we drink and lift up our heads.

Sometimes a brook is more than a friend, a vitalizing teacher. We think of those who at various stages in our careers from childhood on have commanded our admiration, awakened our appreciation, and opened up for us insights into new realms.

Sometimes our Cherith is a book—a book into which, as Mrs. Browning puts it, we "plunge soul-forward, headlong." Charles Darwin tells us:

I never forget that my whole course of life is due to having read and reread as a youth Humboldt's "Personal Narrative."

71

Sometimes the brook is our work which in itself proves our most stimulating refreshment.

"To lie down at night," writes Sir James Stephen, a leader of the English bar a century ago, "to lie down at night with the conviction that since daybreak I had been working harder than any other intellectual operative in London, was among my luxuries."

And when we are sure that the work is something really useful and that we are putting our best into it, there comes

> The unselfish joy which is to helpfulness
> Its own great recompense.

Sometimes the stream is our home, with its confident affection that sends us out of good heart when we leave it, welcomes us back with a restful sympathy, and wherever we are forms a steady current in our being, like Lowell's

> hidden brook
> In the leafy month of June
> That to the sleeping woods all night
> Singeth a quiet tune.

Sometimes our Cherith is the Church in whose fellowship we find our idealism. Her services, the familiar faces of fellow-believers, and phrases of Scripture and hymns with their hallowed associations set flowing heavenly thoughts and feelings and resolves.

Sometimes our brook is a mastering idea that gives existence a new meaning and lights up the horizon with a vision of what should be. We live with this conception, and day after day it proves sufficient for our mental wants. It is to us a river of God full of water.

But our brooks disappoint us by going dry. Friends find their paths moving in different directions and insensibly grow apart. Or death intervenes, and we turn

from a grave saying with Tennyson: "Half my life I leave behind." Or even when we see as much of each other as ever, we come to mean less and less to each other. The spirits of men go solitary ways and only rarely can they move for long together. In the deeper experiences

> Space is but narrow East and West
> There is not room for two abreast.

Revered teachers are outgrown. The man at whose feet we sit with admiring agreement at twenty is judged much more critically by the time we pass thirty. It does not take many years for an inquiring mind to pump dry the brain of a most acute thinker. And even where the exceptional teacher holds his pupils' affectionate honor, death removes the generation of our teachers and leaves us to our own pioneering investigation of life's problems. George Romanes wrote after Charles Darwin's death:

Half the interest of my life seems to have gone when I cannot look forward any more to his dear voice of welcome or to the letters which were my greatest happiness. For now there is no one to venerate, no one to work for, or to think about while working. I always knew that I was leaning on these feelings too much, but I could not try to prevent them; and so at last I am left with a loneliness that never can be filled.

Books, however enriching, do not continue inexhaustible. A few we read several times over. A very choice few we may read every year and find them refreshing and invigorating. But the poets or the novelists or the essayists who are our idols at eighteen are not likely to occupy their niches even a half dozen years later. We may still admire them; we may recognize that we owe them a debt for their contribution at a stage in our development; but our thirst is not slaked by them as it once was.

73

One's work may be a more lasting satisfaction. To some few it is given to find in youth a task at which they are permitted to labor uninterruptedly until death folds their hands. But to most changing conditions, or altered responsibilities, or enfeebled health, put a stop to an occupation which kept the worker's interest.

A church may lose its spiritual appeal. The flow of life in any company of Christians has parched seasons when there is scarcely a trickle in the bed that once contained a torrent. Or the church's waters of life are diverted into side canals of various kinds—controversies, trivial concerns, interests out of line with the heart of Christ—and the household of faith where we used to be sure of renewing our souls no longer restores them.

Even a great idea that enthralled our minds and seemed an illuminating interpretation of the universe after a time ceases to satisfy altogether. No one conception in the mind of man throws light on all the mysteries.

But let us not blame the brook. Perhaps (and here I am discarding the text) there is in it as much water as ever; but our spirits have grown more capacious and are making larger demands. The Cherith by which God had providentially set us no longer answers our need.

And let us remind ourselves that brooks which dry up are part of God's normal training. His Son, Jesus, as well as this ancient prophet, knew the experience of having His brooks fail Him.

Recall the Gospel narrative. Jesus had drunk for months of the friendship of His disciples, particularly of the most congenial three, Peter, James and John. The water of life had been accessible to Him in their loyalty and in their understanding of His purpose. But more than once that brook dried up. "O faithless generation," He said at the foot of the mount of transfiguration, and in Gethsemane He found the dependable three asleep.

His life long He slaked the thirst of His soul from

the Holy Scriptures of His people; and to His last breath their words were on His lips and their inspiration welling up in Him. But there came times when He could not satisfy His thought of God from at least some parts of His Bible. The God of His trust was better than the God on the pages of Moses and the prophets.

His work was a nourishing stimulus; and no wonder, when we recall what He did for men. The ravens that brought Him bread were the helps that He gave other people: "My meat is to do the will of Him that sent me, and to accomplish His work." But His task sometimes failed Him, either because He could do nothing as at Nazareth, or because at the last He had to stop trying to do and let men do to Him as they would. He had to learn that most difficult lesson, that there are situations in which we do most for God when we find ourselves incapable of doing anything, and are forced to be passive and endure what seems defeat and frustration.

His home was a priceless possession from which He drew the words He used for God; and father and mother were to Him sacraments of the Most High. But there came a day when that home failed Him, when He was misunderstood and interfered with, when His family told people that He was out of His mind.

The Church of His nation had been a wellspring of spiritual vitality to Him. We can hardly overestimate what synagogue and temple were to the growing boy. Ideas and sentiments and phrases derived from them were constantly in His thought and on His lips. From them He absorbed the faith and hope and purpose which were the heritage of Israel. But in time that brook went dry. The maturing mind of the young Carpenter found the conceptions taught in the synagogue at Nazareth cramping. He differed violently from the Church's leaders at Jerusalem, and they repudiated Him as an enemy of the faith.

It was part of the education of the Son of God that the brooks of which He drank dried up.

In Elijah's case we can see a reason why this severe lesson was put into the curriculum assigned to him. He thought too much of himself as one apart from other men. At Horeb he told God: "I, even I only, am left." It was not wise that he should possess a private brook which kept flowing while the rest of the country suffered drought. Any blessings which seem personal privileges are perilous. They become barriers preventing our sympathy with the mass of mankind. They may foster conceit and lead us to feel ourselves favorites of Providence. Elijah might have been content to spend his days as a recluse by the Cherith. His flight to Horeb betrays his instinct to get off by himself. It is easy for all of us to stand aside from affairs and become spectators and critics of the ongoings of our time.

When the brook dries up the prophet is involved in the common sufferings of his people. God takes him to the home of the widow of Zarephath where he is made poignantly to feel what others are undergoing. There he learns not only more of the same lesson of God's unfailing care, but also acquires the ability, by no means native to his make-up, to enter into the lives of this woman and her boy, and sharing their supply of God's kindly provision to unite his trust with theirs in social faith in the God of all. This Old Testament believer is taught to use part of the Lord's prayer: "Give *us our* daily bread." Later when Elijah talked too much of himself with his "I, even I only," God assured him that there were seven thousand in Israel as loyal as he. Now he opens for him the experience of finding himself one in the great household of the Father of all.

Religion does not necessarily render believers in God sympathetic and socially-minded. The godly have often been inhuman. They find the Invisible so satisfying that

they are hard to fellow-mortals. To be sure such religion is defective. "The more piety the more compassion" is the terse statement of an old saint. But it requires the failure of the means through which our religious needs are met to force us out to fellow-human beings with whom we discover a truly social religion. The death of someone who has been our chief inspiration admits us to the fellowship of the sorrowing. The break-up of a home has more than once sent a man into the wider circle of his kinsmen in the family of God. It is the cessation of our Cheriths which drives us to Zarephath. We never see the stormy Elijah under such tender circumstances as in this house where the mother is sadly preparing a last meal for herself and her boy before they starve to death.

If the brook had kept on flowing Elijah would have counted on it, and in course of time God, who had brought him there, would have seemed negligible. The means by which God maintains us are always in danger of becoming barriers shutting us from Him. That is why they are seldom permanent. Broken friendships, teachers outgrown, books exhausted, work which goes stale, loved ones removed, interpretations of existence that cease to satisfy—these are God's ways of renewing our sense of need for Him and sending us off to fresh quests. When Jesus found Peter, James and John asleep in the garden, He went away and prayed a second time. Had they been awake and all sympathy, He might not have been forced to further appeals to His Father.

Rarely do we find without seeking. Unless we are asking Him for something, God appears unable to give us His friendship. He is compelled to plan our lives so that we grow thirsty in order that He may satisfy that thirst by His own presence. This is the sequence in the career of this typical workman of God. "And it came to pass after a while, that the brook dried up, because there was

no rain in the land. And the word of the Lord came unto him." An empty stream and an outflow of God's fellowship!

We who live amid the swiftly changing patterns of our kaleidoscopic age receive an unusual amount of the education accorded to Elijah. The books which are the rage for a year or two and sell by the hundred thousand are left to accumulate dust on library shelves. The magazines of a decade ago were filled with articles on topics which no longer arouse public interest. On college campuses one hears the bright youth of 1933 viewing the literary idols of 1920 as obsolete. Fashions of thought and speech change almost as rapidly as fashions in women's clothes. And even the more stable and conservative among us, when we read what we wrote thirty years back, find it hard to think ourselves again into the points of view which were entirely satisfactory to us then.

Thomas Hardy once wrote:

It is the on-going of the world that produces its sadness. If the world stood still at a felicitous moment, there would be no sadness in it. The sun and the moon standing still on Ajalon was not a catastrophe for Israel, but a type of Paradise.

But with due deference to Hardy a stationary heaven or earth would pall in time. Nature in a single season from spring to autumn is forever reminding us by the blooming and fading of her flowers that not the loveliest and most delightful thing is meant to last. With a fine courtesy flowers make room for each other—hepaticas, violets, trilliums, laurel, buttercups, daisies, lilies, gentians, asters—successively giving way to the next group with a gracious *morituri vos salutamus*.

In such a world we are meant to live not regretfully but expectantly. God never deprives us of an inspiration but that He may replace it with another. And in

the development of our spirits the other is always a better. A brook and ravens are not so adequate a disclosure of God's fullness as a mother and child. Is there not a foregleam of Bethlehem in the training of this ancient prophet?

If our loved Cherith dries up, it is only that at some Zarephath God may give us access more fully to Himself with whom is the fountain of life.

IX

FACING EXTINCTION

(An Easter Sermon)

"If it were not so."—John 14:2.

Is IT not a comfort to know that Jesus faced this alternative, that He looked at the possibility of a blank beyond death? "If it were not so."

Eternal life was more indispensable to Jesus than to anyone else. Many persons do not need another life; indeed, they would be at loss to know what to do with it. If a man is leading an animal existence, he can hardly wish it prolonged beyond an animal's term of years. "Let us eat and drink" and tomorrow let us die, for everlasting ages of just eating and drinking would be an insufferable bore. Or if a man fills his days with petty interests none of which satisfy him, why should he want an eternity of futilities? If he is racking his brain to devise methods of "killing time," what prospect could be drearier than to be confronted with the problem of killing eternity? Or if a man cherishes no higher ambition for himself than a successful career, and no hope for others beyond a kindly wish to see them a bit more comfortable, he has no need for deathless life. He can round out any career which he has in mind in one generation, and can satisfy his moderate altruistic feelings in three score years and ten. Immortality would be a questionable blessing.

Not a few thoughtful people have come to realize this,

and they have no passionate longing for another life. They tell you that, while there is an instinctive desire not to drop out of existence altogether, for themselves, they can see no valid reason why they should claim further life; indeed, that it seems presumptuous egotism for any individual to be eager to inflict himself permanently upon the universe. Why should anyone think himself an indispensable factor in the vast scheme of things? If the Christian hope were not so, it would fit in with their outlook upon the world. A man lives on in his influence, in the institutions he has helped to build, in the lives of those whom he has molded, and that seems to them sufficient. They are convinced that the Roman poet, Catullus, was correct when he wrote:

Suns may set and suns upon earth, arise:
As for us, when for us the brief light dies,
There is only night, and an everlasting sleeping.

But everything for which Jesus cared required life beyond death. He spent Himself giving men an ideal which they could not attain within the span of earthly days: "Ye therefore shall be perfect, as your heavenly Father is perfect." He had no illusions as to the rapidity with which men grow. His patience was frequently taxed by those of whom He was most hopeful. "Do ye not yet understand?" "How long shall I be with you?" "Have I been so long time with you, and dost thou not know?" It were a mockery to set before us any such ideal as godlikeness, unless He could assure us of sufficient time in which to achieve it.

We look out on the trees today. There is no lack of energy in the sunlight in mid-April, and every living tree has in it the chlorophyll which answers the descending rays. But we do not expect to see the branches covered with foliage. This is April not June. Jesus believed in the Sun of righteousness shining upon all the sons and

daughters of men; He believed in their capacities to attain characters like their Father's. It is a sublime faith; and unless it be sheer nonsense it presupposes time—time far beyond earth's fleeting years.

A tree in winter with its bare branches held skyward, exposed to gales and to ice, is wistful. It is claiming its kinship with the sun, and asserting its hope of the leafy fullness of summer. If it have imperfections—broken limbs, a trunk which has decayed and been repaired—these are conspicuous. So men appeared to the eyes of Jesus. They had Godward aspirations. They had capacities for fellowship with the Most High. But their misshapen and broken souls were obtrusive. And even when He brought His repair to them, as in the case of the penitent robber at His side on Calvary, the patchwork was noticeable. He did not expect June in January. "Today"—He began to say to that penitent robber, but He said nothing about foliage which covers up scars and conceals distorting damage of storms—"today shalt thou be with Me in paradise." There was capacity in the thief, and the favoring sunlight and warmth of spring with God, and He took it for granted that there was time enough for that penitent bandit to become as perfect as God is perfect. "If it were not so," Jesus' whole career was a mistake. No wonder He looked searchingly at this dark alternative.

Again, Jesus took life very seriously. It might be supposed that those who consider our earthly years all that we possess would prize their every moment more highly than those who fancy that unending æons lie before them. But that is not the case. When once a man is convinced that seventy or eighty years at the outside are all that will ever be his in the ongoings of the universe, they seem to him so trivial in comparison with the vast sweep of the centuries, that it matters little what he does with himself in them. Whenever men have said "Tomorrow

we die," they have played fast and loose with today. Why should they endure a Gethsemane or a Calvary? Why indeed, for these have meaning only against a background of eternity. When they are convinced that for them and for the whole family of mankind life goes on forever and ever, today assumes an august importance. They cannot but use it scrupulously because of its incalculable connections. "I must work the works of Him that sent Me while it is day," for not only the night cometh but momentous tomorrows. If the anguish of the cross can be a ransom for many, it may not be too costly a sacrifice.

A friend once asked the Italian patriot Mazzini, living in exile and poverty and hardship for the sake of the freedom and unity of his country, whether he believed in eternal life.

I do believe—could you doubt it for a moment? That belief is the very soul of all my political, social and religious ideas. The earnestness with which I have endeavored to look at our own terrestrial place of existence, and the feeling of duty which has accompanied me through it, have their root in this belief. The task is here, and the end, or rather the gradual approach to it, cannot be won except by the task being fulfilled. Thence the importance of all the questions concerning our Earth, which is a step on the Jacob's ladder leading to Heaven, a landmark on the journey-road through the Infinite.

If the whole pageant of human existence be a brief episode upon one of the lesser planets to be concluded here, and if your part and mine is a mere wink in the process of the suns, why fool one's self into supposing that it makes much difference what we are or do? Is it surprising that on that night before He underwent the tortures of Golgotha Jesus faced clearly this alternative—"If it were not so"?

Again, Jesus was a venturer. Life meant for Him taking chances. Think of His offering Himself to Jeru-

salem; think of His hazarding death on the cross! But he took these chances always on the assumption of more life in store in which to continue the venture.

Strangely enough there are those who revolt against the Christian hope on the ground that it puts before them a static existence, and they feel that it is nobler and more daring to brush the faith of their fathers aside and sally out into the unknown. Mr. Galsworthy makes one of his characters, a young soldier, say as he dies:

Waste no breath on me—you cannot help. Who knows, who knows? I have no hope, no faith, but I am adventuring. Good bye.

Well, there is precious little opportunity for adventuring in a cemetery. "In my Father's house are many mansions." *There* is limitless scope for enterprise.

Other heights in other lives, God willing.

Yes, God willing, but leave God out, and there are no other heights for so much dust in a graveyard. "Good bye" is just abbreviated "God be with ye."

Jesus was a daring spirit. He was about to take the supreme hazard—to stake everything on laying down His life. Frankly He eyed the possibility of a complete quietus: "If it were not so."

Again, He had spent His days in trying to induce people to love. He was calling those men about the table in the Upper Room "My friends," and asking them to love one another. But what folly to render people more mutually devoted, if a separation is ahead of them, a separation more poignant if they care for each other! It is not everyone with whom one would wish to be forever and ever. Many people see enough of each other in a relatively short while. But when love binds husband and wife, parent and child, brother and sister, friend with friend, human affection raised to the height of Christlike

comradeship—then partings are painful, and a parting forever unendurable. Jesus opens lives to each other, links them by a thousand cords of sympathy and trust. Such relationships cry out for eternity in which to develop and reach fruition. You may recall a thoroughly Christian touch in one of Cowper's letters to Lady Hesketh:

You must know that I should not love you half so well, if I did not believe you would be my friend to eternity. There is not room enough for friendship to unfold itself in such a nook of life as this.

Is it astonishing that as Jesus looked into the faces of these men whom He had attached to Himself so firmly and to whom He had given Himself so devotedly, and knew that the morrow would part them, that He faced afresh this alternative: "If it were not so"?

And once more Jesus' entire career was based on the assumption that this and all worlds were ruled by a loving God. He invariably addressed Him as "Father." He counted Him His chief friend. He knew the reinforcement and guidance and companionship which had come to Him from the Invisible. Could He imagine such a God tossing Him on a rubbish-heap as a discarded tool for which He had no further use?

In one of Jean Paul Richter's stories the narrator sees her mother lying on her death-bed in fear, not because she is to meet a just God, but because she must part with a God she dearly loves. "One friendship perfect and divine" had been her lifelong happiness, and in a few hours it would end. She says good bye to those about her bed, and then exclaims: "Now comes that which is the bitterest—I must take farewell of the most Beloved of all—of Thee, my God."

Instantly one feels that to be forced to say farewell to any such God as Jesus believed in is unthinkable. How could either Father or Son "fare well" robbed of the

other? He is the one inseparable Comrade, so that one can always say: "Adieu—God be with ye."

A friend of Tennyson's records a conversation with him concerning what lies beyond death, in which the poet "crimson with excitement" declared that if immortality "be not true, then no God but a mocking fiend created us," and he added "I'd sink my head tonight in a chloroformed handkerchief and have done with it all."

Suppose when Jesus cried, "Father, into Thy hands I commend my spirit," there was no Father there, but an impersonal Force—the uncaring, unfeeling Order of Things—His life and death were a ghastly blunder. He was pitiably deluded; and with the best of intentions He had deluded others, and He should live in history as the supreme Charlatan. Are we surprised that on the eve of the final commitment of Himself to God, He scanned the alternative: "If it were not so"?

To none other among the dwellers on our planet was a second and an enduring life so essential as to Jesus. Everything for which He cared demanded it. If this basic assumption were not certain to Him, He was not dealing honestly with those who gave Him their confidence. "If it were not so, I would have told you."

But in a matter so vital telling is not enough. What assurance does He give? Listen as He begins: "Let not your hearts be troubled. Believe in God." He had tested that faith all along; now He gives the final demonstration. He is going to a death which His opponents have planned as the effective stop to His career. However you may explain the event which lies behind the narratives with which our Gospels close, the indisputable fact of history is that they did not succeed. Jesus was a more living and more irresistible Factor in Jerusalem, and in the world, subsequent to His death, than He had ever been in the days of His flesh. His confidence in God was gloriously vindicated. Easter, and the millions of Easters

all over the world, generation after generation, in which men experience new life through Christ crucified and buried, this is the earth-wide and ever-repeated corroboration of the faith of Jesus in a God akin to Himself. Outsiders can see that He is not a spent force, but a living Factor in the lives of thousands. But outsiders can never understand what He is as the resurrection and the life. Only insiders, who know this for themselves, are certain that His trust in God was not misplaced, that the universe has refused to bury Him and keep Him buried, and has given Him a resurrection and an abiding power. If Jesus' career had ended in defeat, then we might have concluded that He had been mistaken, that ours is a godless universe. But if, as He confidently expected, His death has given His cause inextinguishable vitality, and He goes His way age after age a Life-giver, then the universe has at its center the God of His faith. "Believe in God" He bids us, and Easter confirms and demonstrates the correctness of His trust.

"Believe also in Me." There is something touching in so sincere a Man's asking friends to have confidence in Him. Can we distrust Him? Is it credible that a life like His was built on a delusion? Can the noblest thing our planet has witnessed—the character of Jesus—have been based on falsehood? Could His words so penetratingly interpret what is in man and continue age after age to furnish the wisest guidance in human affairs, were they embedded in a fallacy? Could His example continue to inspire men of every century and clime and race to their noblest efforts, if His own career had been guided by a mistake? Could His cross lift thousands out of animalism, and thousands more out of despair, and be to this hour the beckoning ideal of the most aspiring nations, if He had gone to His death on a misunderstanding of the ultimate reality behind this and all worlds? What Jesus was and what He has stood for in human

history is the convincing proof that His faith was no delusion. Could a fool accomplish such things?

"In my Father's house are many mansions." If it be so, as believing in God and in Jesus it surely is so, let us tell ourselves again this Easter on what we can count.

With all our hampering faults and hindering weaknesses we can confidently set before ourselves the impossible achievement of becoming godlike. We have time enough: as Lessing said to himself, "Is not all eternity mine?" And we have the reinforcing power of Him who turned the seeming defeat of Jesus into His triumph.

We are justified in taking ourselves and every human being seriously. A college, a home, an industry, a church, a city, is molding characters whose careers are forever.

We are meant to be venturesome, staking all upon love, for a God of love underwrites the risks and guarantees the continuance of the enterprise. Without love's daring we shall not find the many mansions homelike, for they are prepared for such occupants by One who hazarded His all.

We cannot mean too much to each other in this "nook of life." The nook is designed to give such dear personal relations their start. Often we seem a pathetically short time together in it. There are some here for whom this past year has brought desolating separations. And even where persons are spared for years to each other, love is such a growing thing and friendship such a series of rewarding experiences, that partings are not easier, rather harder, after long companionships. We simply cannot do without the Father's house forever; and it is ours and our beloveds' now and always.

And as for our best possession—God known in the face of Jesus—it is not easy to feel at all times that He is here, particularly when events wear a godless look. But remember Good Friday and Easter. Things never seemed blacker than when Jesus of Nazareth bled to

death at Golgotha. He sent His faith up through the dark: "My God, My God." And ever since He has been vindicated. He is our most influential Contemporary today. That is a resurrection in power of which we all are witnesses. And that continuing resurrection is the supremely cogent evidence that His God lives and reigns. You and I can send our hearts up with assurance, saying "Our Father."

"In my Father's house are many mansions. I go to prepare a place for you." We are continually raising the question whether our college years are fitting us for life. Well, here is an abiding life by which college, and whatever education the years beyond afford, must be tested. Think of a life ordered after Christ's taste and judgment, after His conscience and heart: should we fit into it? would it be congenial? should we like it—or rather would it like us?

Physicians not long ago celebrated the anniversary of the death of Thomas Linacre, founder of the Royal College and of famous lectureships at Oxford and Cambridge. When he was sixty years of age, he decided to give up medicine and become a clergyman, and taking up the study of divinity in 1520, he applied himself to the New Testament. When he read carefully the fifth, sixth and seventh chapters of St. Matthew, he threw the book away, and swore that this was either not the Gospel, or we were not Christians.

Well, sit down with these chapters, or with any other section of the Gospels, and look afresh at Jesus Christ as Teacher, Worker, Friend, Sufferer, Lord. Then use the imagination to picture a life which shall exactly suit Him. Are there not some of us who would be so out of place in it and such palpable misfits that we should beg to be put elsewhere? Would not our hell be the appalling sense of unfittedness?

"I go to prepare"—it will be Christlike in every detail.

Could we wish it otherwise? But what of you and me? "I am the resurrection and the life: he that believeth in Me, though he were dead, yet shall he live." That is the Easter which may be ours now—a life committed to Christ, and in His comradeship growing fit for the Master's house here and forever.

X

THE HOME OF SOULS

(A Sermon for Trinity Sunday)

"They said unto Him, Master, where dwellest Thou?
He saith unto them, Come and see."—John 1:38, 39.

ONE never knows a house until one has lived in it. You
may be given a full description by its occupants; you may
be shown photographs of its exterior and interior; you
may examine the architect's drawings, and ask yourself
whether it seems comfortably planned; but you must live
in it to discover the convenience of its arrangements, the
brightness of its rooms, the charm of its outlook, its cool-
ness in summer and its dryness in damp weather, and
find how admirably your family fits into it and how hos-
pitable it proves for the entertainment of your friends.
Living in a house is an exploration. As life's emergencies
arise, the house attests its adaptability or its limitations.

The disciples asked Jesus where He lived, and He invited them to come and see. The narrative concludes with
the heavens open above this Son of man. He lived in God.

This was no new home, but the dwelling-place of believers in all generations. And believers have always found
it hard to tell less religiously inclined fellow-mortals
about the Home of their spirits. They have spoken of its
comfort, of its protection from life's rough weather, of
its refreshment for the tired, of its glorious views, of
its ennobling companionships with the household of the
faithful of all the ages, of its spacious accommodations

for the whole race of mankind, of its surprising welcome for the least fit who seek its shelter, of its beauty, of the unshakable hold it has on the affections and loyalties of all who once live in it. But they have never felt that they could adequately describe it. They end any account of it by saying—"Come and see." Unfortunately in every age many know this Home of the soul only by hearsay, and one never knows a house until he lives in it.

This Dwelling of man's spirit cannot have seemed home to him until he made the discovery that God is one and friendly. To the tribesmen of Africa and the peasants of Korea the invisible is a realm of numberless spirits to be placated. I asked many Korean Christians what most impressed them in their new faith, and almost always came the answer: "That there is one living and true God, and that He is love." To us that appears elementary. We smile at the heathen who talk about the god of war and the god of peace, the god of the hearth and the god of commerce, the god of one's own land and the god of some other folk. But despite our smiles at polytheism, do we find ourselves in the same spiritual atmosphere in war as in peace, in our place of business as with our wife and children, with fellow-countrymen and with foreigners, in our scientific thinking and on our knees in prayer? Do we use the same principles, appeal to the same motives, rely on the same inspirations?

We fancy that we have outgrown the pagan interpretation of our spiritual Home, which saw the unseen world peopled with a discordant company of many gods, as for example in Homer, where one divinity favors the Greeks and another the Trojans, where three jealous goddesses contend for a prize, where one deity is the defender of Achilles and another the patron of Ulysses. But do we not trust and follow one spirit in our families and another in our business dealings, one spirit in our patriotism and another in our feelings towards men of other races,

one spirit in our scientific investigations and another in
our acceptance of religious beliefs? Unconsciously we
slip back into a crude polytheism. We do not feel that
the same Spirit is to be relied on and obeyed in every
sphere of life and in our relations with all men. We do
not believe that the same motives and incentives which
can be used to make a satisfactory home can be trusted
in industry and in statesmanship. Instead of holding with
the seers of Israel to the unity of God, we are back among
the rival divinities who filled the Greek Olympus.

Christianity starts with the parent faith of Judaism in
one God, of whom and through whom and unto whom
are all things. If we adore God as love in our families,
we cannot worship Him as force in international relations, nor as self-interest in commercial dealings, nor
as impersonal energy resident in nature. We cannot
revere Him as truth in our universities and as tradition
in our churches. If to know Him as love is true religion for ourselves and our children, and not too good
to be our religion, then we cannot think that to know
Him as less than love and be frightened or fatalistic
or unhoping is good enough religion for fellow-mortals
in Asia or Africa or here among the millions of this cos-
mopolitan city. Our spiritual home is one God, in whom
we dwell with our nearest and dearest and with men of
other lands and races, one God in whom we have our
friendships, form our opinions on public questions, and
do our business, one God in whom our life is unified—
made all of a piece and all divinely good.

The disciples had believed in the unity of God before
they knew Jesus. How came it that, after knowing Jesus
and living with Him in God, they thought of God as
the Trinity in Unity? Why do modern Christians still
speak of this Triunity in their spiritual Home?

If we dwell spiritually with Jesus, we look up to the
Lord of the universe above and within us as our Father.

We recognize that it is a word borrowed from human life, and that the best father or mother our world has ever seen is an imperfect symbol of the wisdom, the resourcefulness, the authority, the devotion of the Most High to whom we apply this name. But it is the word Jesus found fittest, and in our experience we discover that God is fatherly to those who live with Him in trust. We give Him the confidence, the reverence, the obedience, we should accord the best of fathers, and we do not find it misplaced. "Like as a father, so the Lord." He trusts us as fathers trust their children. And He lives up to His obligations, supplying us with the thoughtful care, the wise guidance, the maturing companionship, which dutiful parents give sons and daughters. Outsiders may deride our faith. They may declare that the Force behind the universe seems an indifferent and ruthless Fate; that there is nothing fatherly about it. We can only reply that one can never know a house until one has made it one's home. Jesus lived in God, and has enabled thousands in every century since to live with Him in God. He and they, down to ourselves, have found fatherhood there.

So remotely conventional a Christian as George Meredith says in a letter:

I hold to the word "Father." No young child can take the meaning of "Spirit." We must give him a concrete form or he will not put an idea in what he is uttering. He must address somebody. Later, when he throws off his childishness, he will, if you are watching and assisting him, learn to see that he has prayed to no false impersonation in addressing an invisible "Father."

Those who have lived with Jesus in God have made a further discovery. They have heard Jesus calling Himself the Son, and while He has called them His brethren, they have found something altogether unique about Him. We have known other men, past and present, in whom

94

we have had glimpses of the divine, but Jesus discloses all we adore in our Father. Spontaneously we find ourselves worshiping Him, and according Him the same loyalty and trust we offer the Most High. Either we are idolaters, or Jesus deserves the same homage and devotion which we yield to God. This does not mean that we are relapsing into polytheism, as the Greeks worshiped Zeus and Athene, and the Romans Mars and Apollo. The first Christians were Jews, believing in one God, but they saw no incongruity in thinking of Jesus as on His throne. Indeed, they could place Jesus nowhere else. In a supreme moment one of them addressed Him: "My Lord and my God." Jesus is for us the unveiling in a completely human life of the God whom He and we adore. There is sonship as well as fatherhood in our spiritual Home, one Son in whom the Father is completely manifested, and who gives Himself as the Elder Brother to all God's other children to lead us into His sonship with the Lord of earth and heaven.

Nor does this exhaust what Christians discover in their spiritual Home. When they live with Jesus in His Father, they find themselves in a life together in which they become new men, are reinforced with courage and patience, are guided by an inward Voice, are filled with an upwelling life—a life akin to the abounding life of Jesus. This indwelling and upsurging and outflowing Life they call the Holy Spirit. If we are correct in worshiping the Father in Jesus, then this Spirit with us is also God.

Let us borrow an illustration from the discoveries of physics. In 1868 Sir Norman Lockyer with the aid of the spectroscope detected on the sun bright jets of gas unlike any known on earth, and gave it the name of Helium. In 1895 Sir William Ramsay found this same gas in tubes with which he was experimenting in his laboratory, and noted that Helium was non-inflammable. During the War a non-inflammable gas was sought as

the fuel for airships, and Helium was discovered in large quantities in certain of our western states and Canada. Today it is employed in all our large airships, enabling them to locate their machinery within the ship, instead of in cars hung beneath it, as in the European airships.

You see the analogy. Men had worshiped a righteous and friendly God in the heavens. They found Him at their side in Jesus. Through Jesus they found Him available as an indwelling Spirit—the light and force of their lives and the corporate possession of the Christian Church. They did not think of Him as three gods, as the Romans placed Neptune beside Jupiter and Juno in their Pantheon. The Trinity was an attempt to combat the polytheism of the pagan world, to assert that God the Home of all devout souls is one, and that in His unity are fatherhood, sonship and indwelling spiritual Life.

If you think of it, in our own homes there are three methods by which our lives are trained. The earliest is *regulation*. A baby's life is planned for him and he lives on a schedule. As he grows there is less regulation and more room for personal initiative. The second is *imitation*. A child is constantly watching older folk and other children and doing as they do. But as he matures, we expect him to be less dominated by the example of others, and to choose his own course. The third is *inspiration*. Boys and girls, men and women, are laid hold on by those who claim their loyalty, and they catch their spirit from them. When father and mother have long ceased to regulate son and daughter, when sons and daughters no longer consciously imitate them, they still live on in the lives that honor and love them.

And we find all three—regulation, imitation, inspiration—in our spiritual Home. As Father God appoints the circumstances under which we live, and to the end of our days we are in a world largely outside our control. We accept its situations from His hand, and trust His

providence. As our Brother in Christ He gives us a life to follow, a faith to share, a devotion to the brotherhood to make ours as He gave Himself for us. Throughout our years that Figure stands before us, beckoning us to become like Him. As the Holy Spirit of the Father and the Son, He more and more possesses us, becoming our inmost Life, the wellspring of motives and sympathies and purposes. By all three processes—regulation, imitation, inspiration—God redeems us to Himself and makes us sharers of His life. We know God as Father, Son and Holy Spirit in our experience of dwelling in Him, the Home of souls.

Theologians, with doubtful success, have tried to carry their explanations further, and tell us how Father and Son and Spirit are related in their spiritual unity. We have always to distinguish between an experience and the explanation of it.

Have you ever looked up the definition lexicographers give us of the verb "to kiss"? Here is what the Century Dictionary says it is:

To smack with the pursed lips (a compression of the closed cavity of the mouth by the cheeks giving a slight sound when the rounded contact of the lips with one another is broken).

Probably that is a correct and orthodox description of a kiss, but what mother would first consult the dictionary and then embrace her baby, or what lover, returning from the momentous experience of being accepted, would find in this definition a satisfactory account of what he had done? Dictionaries are useful volumes in the interest of accurate employment of language. Creeds are useful documents in conserving and clarifying what men have experienced in their life of faith. The statements of the Trinity in Unity preserve what Christians through many generations have discovered who have made their home in God;

but few men have first read the statement and then gone to make the discovery nor, having made the discovery, do they find the statement containing all they have found. Our souls take to God instinctively, as a mother kisses her child or man and maid fall in love. No dictionary can ever tell all that is in a kiss, and no doctrinal statement will ever record what God is to those who love Him. Only those who with Jesus live in Him know.

The practical question for us is whether we avail ourselves of the riches in our spiritual Home. Descriptions suggest what is there. Some persons get much more out of their homes than others; how much are we drawing from the Home of souls?

Do we rely on God's fatherhood, letting Him be the Parent of plans and opinions and interests? Do we defer to His fatherly authority—"Thy will be done"? Do we trust ourselves utterly to His love?

There are many orphan spirits today. Readers of the recently published *Letters of Katherine Mansfield* will recall her wistfulness for God. In her delight in a lovely spot in the Alps she writes:

If only one could make some small grasshoppery sound of praise to someone—thanks to someone, but who?

And in her mood of need she writes again:

It seems to me that there is a great change come over the world since people like us believed in God, God is now gone for all of us. Yet we must believe, and not only that—we must carry our weakness and our sin and our devilishness to somebody.

There is a pathetic orphaned spirit craving a Father. Are you and I thanking Him, confessing to Him, depending upon Him?

Do we use His Self-revealing in Jesus as our invariable thought of Him so that our God is really Christlike? Do we think of Him as giving Himself to and for His

THE HOME OF SOULS

children as Jesus suffered for us at Calvary? Do we expect today the same enriching friendship His disciples found in the Upper Room? Is God in Christ the standard of conduct for us?

Ten years ago George Bernard Shaw wrote in his whimsical way:

I am no more a Christian than Pilate was, or you, gentle reader; and yet, like Pilate, I greatly prefer Jesus to Annas or Caiaphas; and I am ready to admit that after contemplating the world and human nature for nearly sixty years, I see no way out of the world's misery but the way which would have been found by Christ's will, if He had undertaken the work of a modern practical statesman.

Do we obey the unveiling of God's conscience in Christ?

Do we believe in the Holy Ghost—in God present and active within us, supplementing our weakness, enlightening our ignorance, molding our wills, keeping us in unity with lovers of Christ everywhere and equipping us with every grace and gift we need to make our world Christian if we let Him? Are we merely God-seekers, or are we God-possessed, God-led, God-empowered?

To believe in the Trinity is to live with Father, Son and Spirit, and to know what God is to those who trust Him.

It is heartening to recall that as life advances we grow up into an appreciation of the Dwelling-place of our spirits. Heinrich Heine, born a Jew, has put this developing experience into a chapter of autobiography:

Ah, my child, while I was yet a little boy, while I yet sat upon my mother's knee, I believed in God the Father, who rules up there in heaven, good and great; who created the beautiful earth, and the beautiful men and women thereon; who ordained for sun, moon and stars their courses.

When I got bigger, my child, I comprehended yet a great deal more than this, and grew intelligent; and believed on the Son also, on the beloved Son, who loved us and revealed love to us; and for His reward, as always happens, was crucified by the people.

Now, when I am grown up, have read much, have travelled much, my heart swells within me, and with my whole heart I believe on the Holy Ghost. The greatest miracles were of His working, and still greater miracles doth He even now work. He burst in sunder the oppressor's stronghold, and he burst in sunder the bondsman's yoke. He heals old death-wounds and renews the ancient right. All mankind are one race of noble equals before Him. He chases away the evening clouds and the dark cobwebs of the brain, which have spoilt love and joy for us, which day and night have lowered on us.

This is one man's exploration of his soul's Home. One never knows what a house is like until one lives in it. "Master, where dwellest Thou? He saith unto them, Come and see."

HARPERS
MONTHLY PULPIT

A New Departure in Religious Book Publishing

A new series, in which is issued, once each month, a selection of the finest sermons of one outstanding preacher The list of those whose sermons are being published in the series makes up a roster of the great names in American preaching. And press, pulpit, and laity have united in greeting the series as an important new addition to religious book publishing.

Typical press comments on volumes already issued:

"The publishers have picked a dozen of the best preachers and the sermons, to judge by the first volume, will be excellent and representative."—*Herald Tribune.*

"The popular book-of-the-month idea has a new adaptation in the plan of Harper & Brothers to publish regularly, beginning this fall, a monthly volume of sermons. . . . The first two volumes augur well for the series."—*Zion's Herald.*

"The books are readable and attractive in form and will make a splendid body of modern homiletic material in the course of a year."—*Presbyterian Advance.*

"I have just received three volumes of sermons—all from the house of Harper & Brothers—which I have read with great interest and to the confirmation of a conviction I have often voiced, that the days of fine preaching have not passed away."—*Frederick Lynch, Reformed Church Messenger.*

FURTHER DETAILS ON THE FOLLOWING PAGES

WHEN CHRIST PASSES BY
by Walter Russell Bowie

Introduction by Joseph Fort Newton. Any roster of the great preachers of America would place Dr. Bowie high in the list. He is rector of Grace Church, New York, and author of *The Master, When Jesus Was Born,* and many other books. What Dean Charles W. Gilkey calls "his deep religious instincts and his gift of poetic imagination and expression" are revealed at their best in the pages of this book.

THE UNIVERSITY OF EXPERIENCE
by Lynn Harold Hough

Introduction by Reinhold Niebuhr. "Dr. Hough is always looking for a way of uniting the moral passion of the prophets with the astute insights of disciplined minds," says Reinhold Niebuhr. "In this new volume of sermons we have Dr. Hough in his most characteristic contribution to the Christian thought of our day."

BLUNDERING INTO PARADISE
by Edgar DeWitt Jones

Introduction by Gaius Glenn Atkins. Minister of the Central Woodward (Christian) Church, Detroit, Edgar DeWitt Jones is famous far beyond the confines of his own denomination and city. In this, his ninth published work, Dr. Jones proclaims a gospel of social hope and personal power. "What Dr. Jones here writes is telling in topic, original in approach, vital, soundly religious, and substantial," says Gaius Glenn Atkins.

You and Yourself
by *Albert George Butzer*

Introduction by Harry Emerson Fosdick. Acclaimed by Dr. Henry Sloane Coffin and others as one of the outstanding younger preachers of today, Dr. Butzer at present occupies the pulpit of the Westminster Presbyterian Church of Buffalo, one of the outstanding churches of that city and of his denomination. "These sermons . . . come straight out of human experience and snugly fit the thoughts and lives of modern people," says Harry Emerson Fosdick.

Perspectives
by *Charles W. Gilkey*

Introduction by Robert R. Wicks. "The writer's method is poetic and suggestive, reminding us of age-old institutions that have kept our race moving out beyond the paths of least resistance where man's uncertain will is caught and held by loyalty that feels a higher claim than his fellow men can make upon him," writes Robert R. Wicks. Dr. Gilkey is dean of the University of Chicago chapel, although his influence is by no means confined to that pulpit.

The Unemployed Carpenter
by *Ralph W. Sockman*

Introduction by Henry Sloane Coffin. The minister of Christ Church (Methodist Episcopal), New York, attacks problems as realistically as Walter Lippmann or Bertrand Russell, and his clear, incisive prose is a joy to read, as is also evidenced in his *Morals of Tomorrow*. "Dr. Sockman is always interesting, generally picturesque, frequently kindling, and his messages grip intelligence and heart. . . . He is . . . a force for righteousness," writes Henry Sloane Coffin.

Little Evils That Lay Waste Life
by Miles H. Krumbine

Introduction by Lynn Harold Hough. The minister of the Plymouth Church of Shaker Heights, Cleveland, is an outstanding preacher, having achieved considerable renown through his *Ways of Believing* and other writings. Dr. Lynn Harold Hough writes: "You have scarcely read a paragraph in one of his publications before you come upon a quality of clear candor which compels your admiration and commands your respect. . . . The realism of Dr. Krumbine's preaching cleanses the air of the mind. . . ."

The Sensible Man's View of Religion
by John Haynes Holmes

Introduction by Stephen S. Wise. Dr. Holmes has ever been in the forefront of liberal movements for social, political and religious reform. "In my humble opinion," writes Dr. Joseph Fort Newton, "the sermons by Dr. Holmes are the finest and best so far in your series. They are simply tremendous." Rabbi Stephen S. Wise introduces the famous minister of the Community Church of New York as the "most religious of the humanists and the most humanistic of the religionists."

A World That Cannot Be Shaken
by Ernest Fremont Tittle

Introduction by Halford E. Luccock. To Dr. Tittle, brilliant minister of the First Methodist Church, Evanston, Illinois, the field of the pulpit is life—all of life. He has a message for the individual, and for society as well. "His is a poised spirit. . . . In this book, as in all his preaching, there is the vision of a clear, unblinking eye looking out at the world, and the intense feeling of a sensitive heart," says Halford E. Luccock.